The Crypto Revolution

How Blockchain & Bitcoin Are Changing the World

Subhajit Ghosh

The Crypto Revolution
How Blockchain & Bitcoin Are Changing the World

Author: Subhajit Ghosh

Publisher: Self Publish.

First Edition, 2025

DISCLAIMER

This book, "The Decentralized Revolution: How Blockchain & Crypto Are Shaping Our Future" is a deep dive into the world of blockchain, cryptocurrencies, DeFi, AI, and the broader concept of decentralization. It explores how these technologies are transforming economies, governance, and personal freedoms. However, before you proceed, it is important to understand the nature and intent of this book.

This is not a financial, legal, or investment guide. While it discusses the opportunities in Web3, decentralized finance, and digital assets, it does not guarantee financial success or advocate for any specific investment strategy. Cryptocurrencies and DeFi are highly volatile, and the risks involved can be substantial. The author and publisher take no responsibility for any financial losses, legal issues, or personal decisions made based on the contents of this book. Readers are encouraged to consult professional advisors before making any financial or investment moves.

Additionally, technology evolves rapidly. While every effort has been made to ensure the accuracy of the information presented, blockchain, AI, and Web3 are fields that are constantly changing. Some ideas, predictions, or explanations in this book may become outdated as new advancements emerge, regulations shift, and market conditions fluctuate. It is always advisable to verify facts from trusted and updated sources.

This book is not intended as a political statement or an attack on any government, institution, or regulatory authority. It examines decentralization from a technological and philosophical perspective, discussing both its potential benefits and challenges. It does not promote financial anarchy, tax evasion, or illegal activities. Instead, it aims to educate and inspire critical thinking about the future of finance, governance, and personal autonomy in a digital world.

Furthermore, decentralization is not without risks. In a world where individuals have full control over their assets, security becomes a personal responsibility. Losing private keys, falling victim to scams, or interacting with fraudulent projects can lead to irreversible losses. Readers must exercise caution, conduct their own research, and take necessary security measures when navigating the decentralized landscape.

The ideas and concepts in this book are meant to inform, provoke thought, and spark discussion—not to dictate absolute truths or endorse a singular path forward. The future is unpredictable, and the evolution of decentralization will depend on the choices we, as a society, make.

But make no mistake—the world is changing, whether we are ready or not.

The era of centralized control is fading, and the rise of decentralization is no longer a distant theory—it is happening right now, reshaping the very foundation of money, power, and governance. The question is no longer if this revolution will take place. The question is:

Will you be a passive observer of change, or will you take control and become part of it?

The choice is yours.

Welcome to The Decentralized Revolution.

TABLE OF CONTENTS

CHAPTER THREE

THE RISE OF DEFI – A WORLD WITHOUT BANKS?

CHAPTER FOUR

THE GLOBAL ADOPTION CURVE: FROM DOUBT TO DECENTRALIZED REVOLUTION

CHAPTER FIVE

CHAPTER SIX

AI, BLOCKCHAIN & THE NEXT WAVE OF DECENTRALIZATION

CHAPTER SEVEN

THE BATTLE FOR DIGITAL FREEDOM – GOVERNMENTS VS. DECENTRALIZATION

CHAPTER TEN

THE PSYCHOLOGY OF DECENTRALIZATION – ARE HUMANS READY FOR FULL DIGITAL FREEDOM?

CHAPTER ELEVEN

WHAT'S NEXT? PREPARING FOR THE DECENTRALIZED FUTURE

CHAPTER TWELVE

THE FINAL STEP– CAN HUMANITY ACHIEVE FULL DECENTRALIZATION?

ACKNOWLEDGEMENTS

No revolution happens in isolation, and this book is no exception. It exists because of the bold thinkers, relentless innovators, and fearless dreamers who refuse to accept the world as it is—and instead, dare to build something better.

To the pioneers of blockchain and Web3, from Satoshi Nakamoto's mysterious genius to the visionaries shaping DeFi, DAOs, and the Metaverse—your work has ignited a financial and technological revolution that will define the future.

To the Indian blockchain and crypto community, whose resilience and innovation inspire millions—this book is for you. From the developers in Bangalore to the entrepreneurs in Mumbai and the thinkers in Delhi, your contributions are shaping India's role in the decentralized future.

To my friends, mentors, and fellow crypto enthusiasts, thank you for the endless debates, thought-provoking discussions, and the challenges that forced me to think deeper. Your insights have left an undeniable mark on these pages.

To my family and loved ones, your patience and support allowed me to dive headfirst into this world of decentralization. Every late-night research session, every moment lost in thought, and every word written was made possible because of you.

And most importantly, to you, the reader—the explorer, the sceptic, the believer. The decentralized future belongs to those who choose to understand it, shape it, and be part of it. This book is just the beginning of a much bigger journey.

The world is changing. The question is—will you be part of the revolution?

WHY THIS BOOK?

Imagine waking up one morning and discovering that your bank account has been frozen—not because you did anything wrong, but because of a government policy change that happened overnight. Your hard-earned money, which you trusted the bank to protect, is suddenly out of your reach. You scramble to find answers, but all you get is red tape, bureaucratic delays, and the sinking realization that your financial freedom is not truly yours.

Now, imagine you've spent decades saving money, only to realize that inflation has silently stolen its value. What could buy you a home ten years ago can barely get you a small apartment today. The price of everything—food, fuel, education—keeps rising, while your purchasing power keeps shrinking. You worked hard, followed the rules, did everything society told you to do, yet you're still at the mercy of decisions made by banks, politicians, and economic policies beyond your control.

But what if there was another way?

What if you didn't have to rely on banks to hold your money? What if inflation and government restrictions couldn't erode your wealth? What if you could send and receive money without intermediaries, without high fees, and without waiting days for approval? What if your financial future was entirely in your own hands?

This is not some far-fetched dream. This is the decentralized revolution—a shift that is already happening, right now, transforming the way we think about money, power, and governance.

Blockchain, cryptocurrencies, decentralized finance (DeFi), and Web3 are not just trends. They are the building blocks of a new world where individuals regain control, where financial systems operate without middlemen, and where technology empowers the people rather than the institutions that have controlled economies for centuries. But despite its massive potential, most people have no idea what's coming.

Some dismiss it as a bubble. Some fear it. Some believe governments and corporations will shut it down before it truly takes over. But history has shown us that once a technological revolution begins, it cannot be stopped—only delayed. The internet was once feared, mocked, and resisted by traditional industries, yet today, it dominates every aspect of life. The same is happening with decentralization.

And that's exactly why this book exists.

This is not a book filled with dry technical jargon meant only for blockchain developers. It is not a textbook on economics or a theoretical discussion on financial systems. This book is for the dreamers, the sceptics, the curious minds who see cracks in the current system and wonder if there's a better way. It's for those who are tired of:

- Banks and corporations controlling their financial future.
- Governments deciding what they can and cannot do with their own money.
- Social media giants owning their identity, personal data, and digital existence.
- Watching the rich get richer while ordinary people struggle within a rigged system.

If any of this resonates with you, then this book is for you.

This book will help you understand what decentralization truly means—not just in theory, but in practice. You'll learn how blockchain is disrupting banking, how AI and smart contracts are replacing middlemen, how DeFi is enabling financial independence, and how decentralized autonomous organizations (DAOs) are challenging the very concept of corporate hierarchy. You'll see why governments are afraid of this movement, how they are fighting back, and what it means for the future of money and power.

Most importantly, this book is not about speculation. It's about preparation. Because whether you choose to embrace it or ignore it, decentralization will change your life—the only question is whether you'll be ready for it.

Right now, you have two choices.

You can dismiss decentralization, ignore crypto, and believe that banks, governments, and big corporations will always have your best interests at heart. You can assume that the financial system you grew up with will remain unchanged, even as cracks begin to show.

Or you can educate yourself, understand this revolution, and take control of your financial future before it's too late.

This book is an invitation. An invitation to break free from outdated systems, to rethink power, money, and governance, and to become part of the transformation that is already reshaping the world.

Because the truth is simple: The future is no longer in the hands of the few. It is in your hands.

Welcome to The Decentralized Revolution.

The world is changing.

Will you be part of it?

"Bitcoin replaces trust in institutions with mathematical proof. In a world where trust has been broken again and again, that's revolutionary."

©Andreas M. Antonopoulos (Author, Mastering Bitcoin)

CHAPTER ONE

THE END OF TRUST

"When trust in paper fades, money evolves – what once was printed is nowencrypted. The future of value lies not in ink, but in code."

Mumbai, 2035,

The city never sleeps, but it doesn't feel the same anymore. The honking of auto-rickshaws has faded. No one waves cash at street vendors. And banks? Most of them have disappeared.

Anjan steps into a café in Lower Parel, where old textile mills once stood. Now, the area is buzzing with tech startups, blockchain firms, and AI-driven businesses. There's no cashier at the counter—just a sleek screen displaying the price of his filter coffee in Bitcoin, Ethereum, and Digital Rupee (India's Central Bank Digital Currency).

As he scans his crypto wallet, the transaction is completed in an instant. No waiting, no extra fees. Just a simple peer-to-peer transfer verified on the blockchain.

Outside, the cityscape is dotted with billboards advertising tokenized real estate, decentralized investment platforms, and blockchain-powered education systems. Mumbai isn't just the financial capital of India anymore—it's at the heart of the decentralized revolution.

Anjan remembers a time when things were different. A time when sending money to his cousin in Dubai took three days and cost him a 5% bank fee. A time when his parents worried about their savings losing value every year. A time when businesses had to trust banks, middlemen, and regulators to keep their money safe.

That world is changing.

And it all started in the 2020s, when people began to question the very system, they had trusted for generations.

THE EVOLUTION OF MONEY: FROM PAPER TO DIGITAL

For decades, money had been simple. You earned, you saved, you spent. But behind the scenes, it wasn't that straightforward.

Money, at its core, was built on trust—trust that a ₹500 note had value, that a bank would hold your deposits, that the financial system would remain stable.

But what happens when that trust starts to fade?

2008: THE FIRST CRACKS IN THE SYSTEM

In the autumn of 2008, the world watched in shock as the global financial system collapsed in front of their eyes. Banks that had stood for over a century crumbled in a matter of weeks. Stock markets plunged. People lost their homes, their savings, and their trust in the institutions they had always believed were too powerful to fail.

The crisis began with reckless lending by major banks. For years, financial institutions had issued risky home loans to people who couldn't afford them, packaging these loans into complex securities and selling them to investors as safe assets. It was a house of cards built on debt, and when the housing market finally collapsed, the entire system came crashing down.

The consequences were devastating. Millions of people lost their jobs. Families were evicted from their homes. Businesses shut down overnight. And yet, while ordinary citizens suffered, the same banks that had caused the collapse were bailed out by governments, using taxpayer money. Instead of facing consequences, these institutions were deemed "too big to fail," reinforcing the idea that the financial system was designed to protect the elite at the expense of the masses.

This was the moment the first cracks appeared in the system. People began to question everything they had been taught about money, banking, and trust. If governments could print unlimited money to bail out corporations, why couldn't they do the same for ordinary people? If banks could take reckless risks and never be held accountable, what did that mean for the future of finance?

But amidst the chaos, a revolution was quietly taking shape.

On October 31, 2008, as the world reeled from the collapse, an anonymous figure—or group—going by the name Satoshi Nakamoto published a white paper titled "Bitcoin: A Peer-to-Peer Electronic Cash System." This document laid out a radical new idea: a financial system that operated without banks, governments, and middlemen. A system where people could store, send, and receive money without trusting any central authority.

At the time, few people realized how significant this was. Most dismissed Bitcoin as an experiment, a passing trend. But in reality, it was the birth of a financial revolution. It was the first glimpse of a future where money was no longer controlled by the same institutions that had failed the world.

2008 was not just the year the financial system broke—it was the year a new system began to rise from its ashes.

The first cracks in the old world had appeared. And from those cracks, decentralization was born.

2016: DEMONETIZATION – WHEN CASH BECAME WORTHLESS OVERNIGHT

On the evening of November 8, 2016, millions of Indians gathered around their televisions as Prime Minister Narendra Modi made a stunning announcement: ₹500 and ₹1,000 notes—the two highest denominations of Indian currency—would no longer be legal tender, effective immediately.

In that single moment, 86% of the country's cash supply became worthless.

Panic erupted. People rushed to ATMs and banks, desperate to exchange their old notes for new ones. Long queues stretched for hours, and cash shortages became widespread. Businesses halted. Daily wage earners found themselves without a means to buy food. The informal economy—heavily reliant on cash transactions—suffered immensely. It was as if money itself had suddenly ceased to exist.

The government justified demonetization as a bold move to curb black money, eliminate counterfeit currency, and push India towards a cashless economy. But the reality was far more complicated. While some illegal cash holdings were indeed wiped out, a vast majority of the demonetized money—over 99%—was eventually deposited back into banks, proving that the measure did little to uncover hidden wealth.

But the real impact of demonetization wasn't just financial—it was psychological.

For the first time, ordinary citizens realized that money was not truly theirs. The cash in their hands—something they had earned, saved, and trusted—could be rendered useless overnight by a government decision. People saw firsthand how centralized control over money meant that policies, not individual choices, determined financial security.

This event also accelerated India's digital payments revolution. UPI (Unified Payments Interface) transactions surged, mobile wallets like Paytm became household names, and banks aggressively pushed cashless transactions. The government's vision of a "Digital India" was set in motion—but at the cost of trust in traditional financial systems.

For many, demonetization was a wake-up call. It made people question:

- If the government could invalidate cash overnight, what stops them from controlling digital money in the future?
- If bank withdrawals could be limited, how much financial freedom do we really have?
- If central banks could print money at will, how safe are our savings from inflation?

These were not just theoretical concerns. They were real-life fears that pushed many Indians to explore alternative financial systems—especially Bitcoin and cryptocurrencies. In the months following demonetization, India saw a massive rise in crypto adoption. People began to see Bitcoin not as just an investment, but as a hedge against monetary policies that could change overnight.

Demonetization did not kill cash—but it planted the seeds of a decentralized revolution in the minds of millions. It proved that money controlled by governments could be taken away at any moment, but money controlled by code, cryptography, and decentralization could offer true financial independence.

In that moment, the foundations of a cashless India were laid.

But alongside it, the desire for a government-free, censorship-resistant financial system was born.

2020: THE RISE OF DIGITAL PAYMENTS & CRYPTO CURIOSITY

The 2020s marked a turning point in how people viewed money, payments, and financial independence. What had once been seen as futuristic or even unnecessary—digital currencies, borderless payments, and decentralized finance—was now becoming a reality. The world was moving toward a cashless society, and for the first time, traditional banking was no longer the only option.

The decade started with the COVID-19 pandemic, an event that accelerated the adoption of digital transactions like never before. As countries went into lockdown, businesses shut down, and economies froze, people had to find new ways to transact without physical cash. Contactless payments, UPI in India, PayPal, Apple Pay, and crypto wallets surged in popularity. Digital payments were no longer just convenient—they became essential.

But alongside the rise of digital banking, something else was happening: people were beginning to question the financial system itself. Governments around the world were printing trillions of dollars to stimulate their economies, but this came at a cost—inflation soared, and the value of fiat currencies began to decline. Suddenly, Bitcoin, once dismissed as a speculative asset, started to look like digital gold.

By 2021, companies like Tesla, MicroStrategy, and Square were adding Bitcoin to their balance sheets. Celebrities and billionaires openly supported crypto, and mainstream investors were starting to pay attention. El Salvador made Bitcoin legal tender, a historic move that signalled the beginning of national adoption. At the same time, the rise of DeFi (Decentralized Finance) and NFTs (Non-Fungible Tokens) brought even more people into the crypto space.

India was no exception. Despite regulatory uncertainty, crypto trading surged, with millions of Indians investing in Bitcoin, Ethereum, and other digital assets. The popularity of UPI (Unified Payments Interface) in India proved that people were ready for instant, digital transactions—paving the way for future blockchain-based payment systems. Meanwhile, startups in Bangalore and Mumbai were building the foundations for Web3, pushing India to the forefront of blockchain innovation.

Governments, however, were beginning to push back. They realized that if crypto adoption continued, they could lose control over monetary policy and financial oversight. Some nations banned or restricted crypto, while others explored Central Bank Digital Currencies (CBDCs)—government-issued digital money that could replace physical cash but remain under central authority. The battle between decentralization and regulation had begun.

2025: THE GREAT CURRENCY DEVALUATION -- A TURNING POINT FOR MONEY

Mumbai, 2025,

Anjan walked into his favourite café in South Mumbai, ordering the same cappuccino he had been drinking for years. But today, something felt different. As he tapped his phone to pay, he noticed the price had nearly doubled compared to last year.

Inflation had always been there—gradual, creeping, silently eating away at purchasing power. But in 2025, things had escalated beyond control.

Over the past year, inflation had surged into double digits in many countries. The U.S. dollar, once considered the safest asset in the world, had lost significant value after years of aggressive money printing. In Europe, protests had erupted in response to rising prices, and governments had imposed capital controls to slow the outflow of money. Emerging economies, like Argentina and Turkey, were facing currency collapses, with citizens rushing to trade their local money for anything more stable—gold, U.S. dollars, or increasingly, Bitcoin and stablecoins.

India was feeling the pressure too. The rupee had depreciated sharply, and everyday expenses—groceries, rent, fuel—had become painfully expensive. The Reserve Bank of India (RBI) had introduced measures to stabilize the economy, including pushing for faster adoption of the Digital Rupee (CBDC) as a means of controlling inflation. But many questioned whether this new government-backed digital currency was truly a solution—or just a way to monitor and restrict transactions more tightly.

Anjan scrolled through his phone, reading headlines from around the world. The pattern was clear:

- ❖ Governments were printing more money to "solve" economic crises.
- ❖ Banks were imposing withdrawal limits to prevent capital flight.
- ❖ People were turning to decentralized alternatives to protect their wealth.

At first, most governments downplayed the impact of crypto. But now, small businesses and freelancers in India were quietly moving to stablecoins and Bitcoin to escape currency devaluation. Even the shop next to the café had a handwritten sign:

“USDT & Bitcoin accepted here.”

For years, people had trusted banks, central banks, and financial institutions to maintain stability. But trust was fading.

The Great Currency Devaluation of 2025 wasn’t just about economics. It was about people waking up—realizing that money, in its traditional form, was no longer something they could rely on. For the first time, ordinary citizens had a choice.

Would they continue depending on a system that had repeatedly failed them?

Or would they opt out and take control of their own financial future?

Anjan took another sip of his cappuccino, glanced at the price tag once again, and made a decision.

Maybe it was time to start paying in Bitcoin.

Maybe it was time to prepare for a new financial era.

The revolution wasn't coming.

It was already here.

THE BIRTH OF A NEW SYSTEM

In 2009, an anonymous figure named Satoshi Nakamoto launched Bitcoin with a simple message hidden in its first block:

"The Times 03/Jan/2009 Chancellor on brink of second bailout for banks."

It was a warning. A statement. And a promise.

Bitcoin wasn't just another currency—it was a financial revolution.

For the first time in history, money was:

- **Decentralized** – No government could print or control it.
- **Transparent** – Every transaction was recorded on the blockchain.
- **Borderless** – It could be sent anywhere in the world, instantly.

At first, Bitcoin was an experiment. Then came Ethereum, unlocking the power of programmable money through smart contracts. Soon, decentralized finance (DeFi) emerged, enabling lending, borrowing, and investing without intermediaries. The explosion of DAOs (Decentralized Autonomous Organizations) proved that even companies could function without CEOs or corporate boards.

By the late 2020s, this new system wasn't just an idea—it was a fully functional parallel economy.

Bitcoin had become digital gold, a hedge against inflation and financial instability. DeFi protocols were processing billions in transactions, replacing banks entirely. NFTs and tokenized assets had revolutionized ownership, from art to real estate. Web3 identity systems allowed people to own their data, breaking free from Big Tech control.

Governments and banks had tried to resist, imposing regulations, bans, and capital controls. But decentralization wasn't a company they could shut down. It wasn't a protest they could silence. It was a movement, a technology, a revolution—one that belonged to the people.

By 2035, decentralized finance (DeFi) platforms, tokenized assets, and smart contracts had reshaped the global economy.

The birth of this new system wasn't loud. There were no riots, no revolutions in the streets. It was happening silently, block by block, transaction by transaction, mind by mind.
The world was changing—not because people demanded it, but because they had discovered something better.

The birth of decentralization wasn't an event.
It was an evolution.

And by now, it was unstoppable.

2035: A NEW FINANCIAL REALITY

Imagine,

Anjan walks down Marine Drive, watching digital billboards display live crypto prices instead of stock market indices.

In a café nearby, an independent artist from Kolkata is minting her latest artwork as an NT, selling it to a collector in Singapore without needing a gallery or middleman.

In a small town in Uttar Pradesh, a farmer is using blockchain-based smart contracts to sell his produce directly to buyers—ensuring fair payments without delays or corruption.

The world has changed.

Money is no longer just paper controlled by governments. It is digital, decentralized, and accessible to all.

The revolution is no longer coming.

It is already here.

*****

"We have elected to put our money and faith in a mathematical framework that is free of politics and human error."

©Tyler Winklevoss (Co-founder, Gemini)

CHAPTER TWO

BITCOIN – THE NEW GOLD STANDARD?

"Bitcoin is a far better store of value than fiat currency."
– Elon Musk

Varanasi, 2035,

The ghats of the Ganges River have seen centuries of change. Kings and dynasties have come and gone. Empires have risen and fallen. But through it all, one thing has remained constant—gold.

For thousands of years, gold has been the ultimate store of value in India. From temples to family heirlooms, from wedding gifts to financial security, it has symbolized wealth, stability, and trust.

But in 2035, things look different. At a local jewellery store near Dashashwamedh Ghat, a young couple is finalizing their wedding shopping. But instead of buying traditional gold jewellery, they are purchasing tokenized gold on the blockchain—digital assets backed by real gold reserves.

The store owner, an elderly man who once swore by physical gold, has adapted to the times. "People still love gold," he says with a smile, "but they also want something more portable, more secure. Many now see Bitcoin as the new gold."

It's a statement that would have been laughed at two decades ago.

But today, it's a reality.

WHY WAS GOLD ALWAYS CONSIDERED THE ULTIMATE ASSET?

For centuries, gold was money.

Long before paper currency existed, kingdoms and civilizations relied on gold because it had unique properties that no other material had:

- **Scarcity** – There was only a limited amount of gold on Earth.
- **Durability** – It never rusted, decayed, or lost its shine.
- **Universal Value** – Every culture, from ancient India to medieval Europe, valued gold.

It was the backbone of the global financial system for over 5,000 years. Even in modern India, families passed down gold not just as jewellery but as generational wealth.

But then, something changed.

Unlike gold, Bitcoin wasn't locked away in vaults or mined from the earth. It was mined by machines, verified by math, and accessible to anyone with an internet connection. It could be sent across the world in seconds. It didn't tarnish, couldn't be counterfeited, and didn't rely on the trust of a government or central authority.

As the global economy continued to feel the aftershocks of the Great Currency Devaluation, a new question began circulating in both financial and political circles:

"Has Bitcoin become the new gold standard?"

CAN BITCOIN REALLY REPLACE GOLD?

To those raised on the legacy of gold—especially in a country like India, where gold isn't just wealth but culture, tradition, and pride—that idea feels almost blasphemous. Gold is physical. You can touch it, wear it, gift it during weddings, pass it down to your children. It has history. It's lasted centuries, survived empires, and held its ground through wars, recessions, and revolutions.

So how can lines of code—even ones as elegant and robust as Bitcoin—compare?

But then again, we live in a world where value is increasingly digital. Our salaries arrive as numbers in a bank app. Our friendships exist on screens. Our businesses run in clouds. And now, our money is evolving too.

Anjan, like many others in his generation, grew up watching his parents buy gold as a sacred form of security. His mother still wore a heavy gold chain gifted by her parents on her wedding day. His father used to remind him that in times of crisis, "gold will never fail you."

But Anjan had seen something else.

He saw friends lose their savings during the 2020 pandemic when the market crashed and panic swept the globe. He watched governments around the world print trillions in stimulus, trying to rescue the economy—only to push inflation higher in the long run. He witnessed his own purchasing power shrink, slowly and silently, while his bank savings grew by a meagre 2–3%.

Then he discovered Bitcoin.

At first, it was curiosity. Then research. Then a cautious investment. But over time, it became something more than just a line item in his portfolio. Bitcoin became a philosophy—a way to opt out of a system he felt increasingly disconnected from.

Because Bitcoin didn't promise safety. It demanded responsibility. It wouldn't bail him out, like a government could—but it wouldn't betray him either.

There were no banks to freeze his funds. No inflation to eat away at his earnings. No overnight policy changes that could limit his access. Just him, his wallet, and a system that treated every participant equally—whether they were a millionaire in New York or a chaiwala in Nagpur.

And that felt powerful.

The deeper Anjan went, the more he realized Bitcoin wasn't trying to *be* gold—it was trying to be something more. Something built for a generation that didn't want vaults and middlemen. A generation that wanted control, portability, and purpose.

Unlike gold, Bitcoin didn't require storage, guards, or appraisal. It didn't require approval from a jeweler or trust in a bank. You could hold it on a USB-sized device or even memorize a seed phrase and carry it across borders, beyond governments and regulations. It wasn't just unseizable—it was untouchable.

In countries like Venezuela, Nigeria, Turkey, and even pockets of India, Bitcoin wasn't being used because it was trendy—it was being used because people had no other choice. Their currencies had failed. Their banks were unreliable. Their governments were unstable. And when systems break down, people fall back on what they trust.

And more and more, that trust was shifting from institutions to code.

Of course, Bitcoin isn't perfect. It's volatile. It's still evolving. It requires a learning curve. Scams happen. Wallets get lost. It doesn't carry the emotional weight that gold does in Indian households—

yet. But neither did the internet, when it first arrived. Neither did mobile phones. Neither did online payments. All of those technologies were once doubted, dismissed, and feared. Until one day, they weren't.

Bitcoin is on the same trajectory—not as a replacement for all money, but as an alternative system. One that gives people a choice. One that doesn't inflate on command. One that doesn't require middlemen. One that is open, borderless, and permissionless.

And perhaps, that's what makes it the "new gold standard."

Not because it replaces gold, but because it replaces the need for trust.

Gold relies on vaults and human systems to maintain its value. Bitcoin relies on math and decentralization. And in a world, that's seen enough manipulation, enough crises, enough broken promises from the very institutions meant to protect us—math is starting to feel a lot more trustworthy than men in suits.
As Arvind looked back at his phone, he didn't see a price chart anymore. He saw resilience. He saw freedom. He saw a digital asset that didn't ask him to believe in politicians, bankers, or broken systems.

> *In the vaults of old wealth, gold still shines. But in the hands of the new generation, Bitcoin glows—with belief.*

It just existed. On the blockchain. Immutable. Unstoppable. Available 24/7, 365 days a year, to anyone in the world.
That's not just an asset. That's a signal. A sign that the rules of money are changing.

He imagined his future child asking, "Dad, why did people trust banks to hold all their money back then?" and smiling as he answered, "We didn't know we had a choice."

But now we do.
So, is Bitcoin the new gold standard?

It may not wear the crown yet. But make no mistake—it's already being weighed, measured, and trusted in a way no digital asset ever has.

THE FALL OF THE GOLD STANDARD - WHEN MONEY BECAME AN ILLUSION

Delhi, 2026,

Madhab uncle still remembers how, in his childhood, a ₹10 note could buy a full bag of ration. His father used to bring home sacks of rice and dal, all bought in cash, with money that felt like it held real weight. Back then, people didn't trust banks too easily. Instead, they trusted something far older, far more Indian—gold.

It was in every household. Worn as jewellery, hidden in lockers, or buried in the back of steel cupboards. It wasn't just an investment. It was a symbol of security, passed down through generations with pride. Families didn't say "save money"; they said "sone mein paisa lagao."

But somewhere along the line, money changed.

And the turning point, though it happened far away—in Washington, D.C., in 1971—would silently alter the financial destiny of families in Mumbai, Patna, Kochi, and every corner of India.

WHEN MONEY LOST ITS SOUL

In 1971, U.S. President Richard Nixon made a quiet announcement that shook the global economy: the United States was officially cutting the link between the dollar and gold. Up until then, the world's currencies, including the Indian Rupee indirectly, were connected to the U.S. dollar—which itself was backed by gold. It gave money meaning. A kind of honesty.

But that night, the U.S. declared it would no longer allow conversion of dollars to gold. That simple policy shift meant that the global financial system—built for centuries on the strength of physical value—was now based on nothing but trust.

India, like most countries, followed the global financial structure. And over the years, the Rupee too became a fully fiat currency—not backed by gold, not backed by assets, but simply by faith in the government's promise.

In the decades that followed, India's economy evolved. The country liberalized in 1991. Technology boomed. Urban life became fast-paced and digital. But through all of this, the currency we used daily was increasingly disconnected from anything tangible.

People didn't notice at first. ₹100 still looked like ₹100. But its buying power quietly weakened every year.

Madhab uncle's ₹10 could once buy a meal for four. Today, ₹100 barely buys a snack. And it's not just nostalgia—it's inflation, the invisible thief.

And what causes it? Among many things, governments printing more and more money.

In India, just like elsewhere, the Reserve Bank of India (RBI) can print currency notes as needed. During economic slowdowns, global pandemics, or political shifts, money supply is increased—but the amount of goods in the market doesn't always increase alongside it. Result? More money chasing fewer goods. Prices rise. Value falls.
This is the downside of fiat currency: it's limitless in supply but limited in worth.

India never officially adopted a gold standard like the U.S. did—but for centuries, gold functioned as the people's reserve currency. When trust in the rupee dipped, Indians quietly turned to what they had always believed in: gold biscuits, sovereign gold coins, temple donations, and bridal jewellery.
But storing wealth in gold had limitations. It's not easy to spend. It's not divisible. It can be stolen. And in modern trade and finance, it doesn't move fast enough. That's when Indians had to rely more on fiat money—even though its foundation was increasingly uncertain.

And after decades of quietly observing its erosion, today's generation is finally asking:

If the rupee isn't backed by gold or any physical asset, then what is it backed by?

MONEY AS ILLUSION

The more you examine it, the more money begins to look like a collective illusion. The ₹500 note in your hand isn't backed by gold stored in RBI's vault. It's backed by trust—in the government, the central bank, and the system. If that trust weakens, so does the value of the note.

This is why economic instability, political tension, or policy changes can cause currency crashes in countries. In extreme cases—like Zimbabwe or Venezuela—money has become so worthless that it's used more as paper than currency.

In India, we haven't reached that point, but the signs are there:

- Rising inflation
- Growing income inequality
- Currency depreciation
- People losing faith in traditional savings

Many Indians are now rethinking what wealth actually means. They're investing in digital assets. Buying gold digitally. Experimenting with Bitcoin and stablecoins. The younger generation is waking up to the idea that if money can be printed endlessly, its value is just as easily diluted.
After the fall of the gold standard, the world shifted to a model where trust is everything.

But now, people are asking: trust in whom?

In a country where scams, inflation, and policy U-turns aren't uncommon, trust can feel like a fragile thing. And in that vacuum, people are searching for financial systems that offer transparency, scarcity, and control.

Some are going back to gold. Others, particularly the digitally native youth, are going to Bitcoin—a currency not tied to any government, not vulnerable to inflation, and capped forever at 21 million units.

Bitcoin may be too volatile today for some, but it represents something people are hungry for—a return to real value, backed not by promises, but by code, math, and consensus.

THE ILLUSION CONTINUES—BUT EYES ARE OPENING

The fall of the gold standard didn't destroy the world. It just changed the game. And for a while, people played along. But as the illusion of money becomes more visible—as rupees buy less, savings earn little, and inflation eats quietly—more Indians are beginning to ask the uncomfortable question:

Is the money in my wallet real? Or is it just paper backed by hope?

Madhab uncle may still keep gold in his locker.

But his nephew? He just bought his first satoshis.

The times are changing.

The illusion is fading.

And the search for something real has begun.

BITCOIN: DIGITAL GOLD? OR SOMETHING MORE?

Varanasi, 2027,

On the ghats of the Ganges, as the morning aarti filled the air with devotion and ancient rhythm, 23-year-old Manash sat with a laptop, sipping masala chai. He wasn't trading stocks or browsing social media. He was checking his Bitcoin node, running live from his solar-powered home in a village just outside the city.

To the people around him, it looked like he was doing something futuristic. But to Aayush, this had already become routine. He wasn't just holding Bitcoin. He was part of the network.

It wasn't just an investment. It wasn't just a hedge against inflation.

It wasn't just digital gold.

It was something more.

More Than Just Gold in a Digital Shell...

For over a decade, Bitcoin has been called "digital gold"—a compliment and a limitation in the same breath.

Yes, Bitcoin shares many traits with gold. It is scarce—only 21 million will ever exist. It is mined, though digitally. It's not

Why Bitcoin Feels Like Digital Gold

Limited supply = Scarcity = Higher value over time.

Immune to inflation and currency manipulation

Globally accepted as a store of value

*Run by **code**, not **central banks***

More secure than any physical vault

controlled by any government. It doesn't rust, doesn't inflate, and cannot be printed on demand like fiat currencies.

In countries like India, where gold has long been a symbol of wealth, status, and intergenerational security, the comparison was clever. It helped explain Bitcoin's core strength: store of value.

But if we stop there, we completely miss the point.
Gold sits in lockers. It waits passively. You can't program it. It doesn't move across continents in seconds. It doesn't care about networks, identities, or freedom.

Bitcoin does.

Bitcoin is not just digital gold. It is digital rebellion, digital sovereignty, and possibly the foundation of a new financial operating system.

THE TECHNOLOGY OF TRUST

Gold has always had value because it was rare and universally recognized. But its limitations are obvious in today's digital world. Try sending gold to someone across the globe. Try breaking it into exact decimals for a payment. Try proving its authenticity instantly.

Bitcoin solved all that.

With Bitcoin, you don't need to trust a middleman. Not a bank, not a corporation, not even a government. The network verifies itself. Every transaction, every coin, every block is etched into a permanent, public, incorruptible ledger.

For the first time in history, trust has been transferred from institutions to code.

That alone makes it more powerful than gold. But Bitcoin didn't stop there.

Bitcoin isn't just money.

It's programmable money. This isn't just about storage—it's about interaction.

With Bitcoin, you can:

- Lock it in a smart contract that releases only when conditions are met.
- Send it to someone without asking anyone for permission.
- Divide it down to one hundred million units (called satoshis) for microtransactions.
- Build systems, games, payment apps, even political movements on top of its protocol.

Gold can't do that. Rupees can't do that. Not even digital UPI can do that without a bank watching.
Bitcoin introduces a new language of financial freedom—one that speaks to the unbanked, the oppressed, the digitally connected, and the globally ambitious.

In rural Tamil Nadu, a girl with a smartphone and no bank account can now receive value from anywhere in the world—without anyone's permission. In Kashmir, someone can store their life's savings in Bitcoin without fear of confiscation or freezing. In urban Mumbai, young freelancers are choosing to get paid in Bitcoin because they trust math over middlemen.

A WEAPON AGAINST INFLATION

Gold has historically been a hedge against inflation. When fiat currencies weaken, gold rises. But Bitcoin takes this protection a step further.

Its supply is hardcoded. Not estimated. Not adjustable. Not politically manipulated. Every ten minutes, a new block. Every four years, a halving. And in 2140, the final coin will be mined.

That predictability is revolutionary in a world where central banks flip policies like switches, where currencies collapse from bad governance, and where common people pay the price.

In India, where inflation eats into savings, fixed deposits offer less than real returns, and the rupee has weakened steadily against the dollar for decades.

Bitcoin offers something rare:

"A fixed supply in an unpredictable world".

FREEDOM IN THE FORM OF CODE

More than anything, Bitcoin is freedom technology.

It gives people control over their wealth—something most of us didn't realize we lacked until we started to lose it.
When the Indian government demonetized ₹500 and ₹1000 notes in 2016, people lined up outside ATMs overnight. When the pandemic hit in 2020, financial dependence became more obvious—people couldn't send money easily, access cash, or control interest rates. And in 2025, during the currency devaluation, many saw their savings lose purchasing power almost silently.

But Bitcoin doesn't ask for permission. It doesn't follow business hours. It doesn't discriminate between rich and poor, urban or rural, Indian or foreign.

If you have a smartphone, you can use Bitcoin. If you have an idea, you can build on Bitcoin. If you have a voice, you can protect it through Bitcoin.

Bitcoin is not just an asset—it's a platform. It's not just a safe haven—it's a revolution.

WHY THIS MATTERS NOW, MORE THAN EVER

We're entering an era where value is digital, trust is decentralized, and borders are blurring.

Gold will always have a role in culture and tradition. But Bitcoin belongs to the future.

It's already being held by countries, traded by institutions, used by refugees, and adopted by communities. It's the financial internet. And just like the internet, most people won't understand its potential—until it becomes unavoidable.

In India, where financial systems are still developing, where young people are globally connected but locally restricted, where innovation is booming but regulation lags behind—Bitcoin fits naturally.
It speaks the language of youth, of speed, of transparency. It's not held back by caste, class, or city. It is an equalizer.

So, is Bitcoin digital gold?

Yes—and far more.

Gold represents preservation. Bitcoin represents possibility.

Gold protects your past. Bitcoin secures your future.

Gold is stored. Bitcoin is used.

Gold sits in vaults. Bitcoin moves at light speed, on a global, borderless, permissionless network.

To call Bitcoin "digital gold" is safe. But the truth is bolder.

Bitcoin is not just the next version of money—it is a rewrite of money's meaning.

And as Manash sat beside the holy river, running his node, sending satoshis, and watching the morning sun rise, he wasn't just participating in an economy.

He was helping build a new one.

One block at a time.

One satoshi at a time.

One belief at a time.

The future doesn't need banks.

It needs belief—and Bitcoin has it.

THE SHIFT: FROM CENTRAL BANKS TO CRYPTO RESERVES

New Delhi, 2032,

In the heart of Lutyens' Delhi, inside an imposing sandstone building, the Reserve Bank of India was holding an emergency meeting. The agenda? Capital flight. But not to Switzerland or Singapore. This time, wealth wasn't being moved in suitcases or offshore accounts. It was disappearing into something far more elusive—crypto wallets.

While governors debated how to restore faith in the rupee, outside on the streets of India's tech cities, a very different conversation was happening. Young entrepreneurs were discussing which stablecoin to hold their business revenue in.

Freelancers in Jaipur were comparing DeFi yields. Farmers in Andhra Pradesh were learning to accept USDT for direct grain payments, bypassing middlemen.

And most notably, state-level governments were quietly exploring whether they too should hold a portion of their budget reserves in Bitcoin or Ethereum, just to hedge against the slow decline of fiat value.

What was once unthinkable was becoming inevitable. The shift had begun.

The world was moving—from central bank-backed reserves to crypto-based stores of value.

HOW DID WE GET HERE?

To understand this seismic shift, we have to go back to the core purpose of a central bank reserve. Traditionally, countries hold reserves—usually in gold or foreign currencies like the US dollar or euro—to maintain economic stability, settle international trade, and back their own currency's strength.

India, for example, holds a mix of gold, foreign currencies, and bonds as its official reserves. These assets act as a financial cushion in case of global shocks.
But here's the catch:
These reserves are subject to political influence.

Fiat currencies like the dollar or euro are inflated over time.

Gold is illiquid and difficult to move during crises.

U.S. Treasury bonds, once considered the safest asset, are now linked to rising U.S. debt.

Add to that a growing trend of financial weaponization—where countries can have their assets frozen, accounts seized, or access to the global financial system revoked due to political tensions.

When Russia was cut off from SWIFT in 2022 and had hundreds of billions in reserves frozen overnight, many governments around the world took note. If that could happen to a major power, what's really safe anymore?

The illusion of stability began to crumble.

CRYPTO AS A STRATEGIC RESERVE

At first, Bitcoin was laughed at. Then it was feared. Now, it's being quietly studied by central banks and treasuries as a serious asset class.

Bitcoin's properties are uniquely suited for the role of a reserve:

- **Fixed supply (21 million)** – Impossible to inflate.
- **Decentralized** – No government controls it.
- **Borderless and liquid** – Can be moved across the world instantly.
- **Transparent** – The ledger is open for all.
- **Resilient** – Has survived crashes, bans, hacks, and continues to thrive.

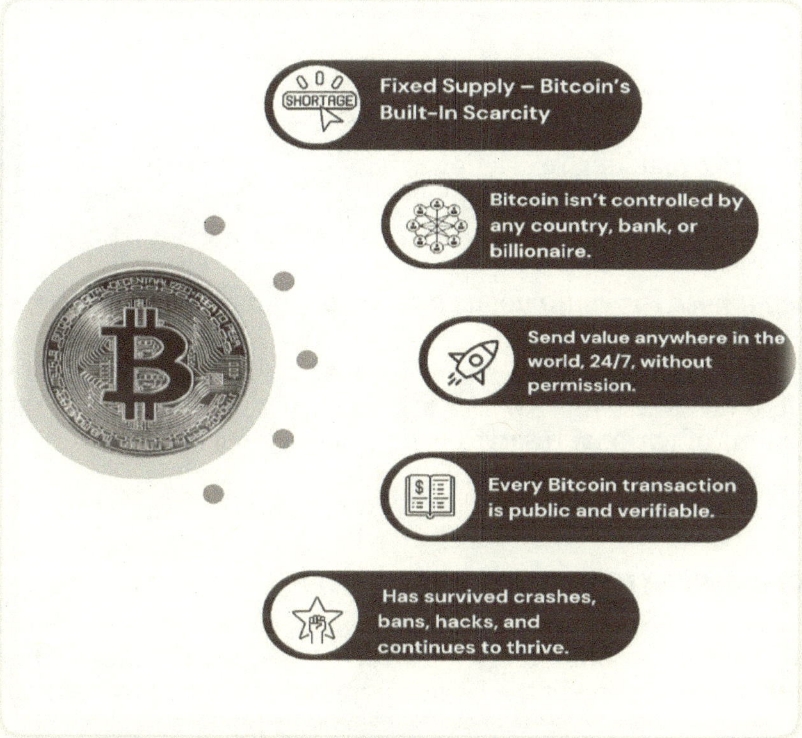

What gold was to the 20th century, *Bitcoin is becoming to the 21st.*

And not just Bitcoin. Stablecoins like USDT and USDC are pegged to the dollar but offer a faster, more efficient, programmable version of fiat. Many institutions and even some governments are realizing:

It's safer to hold stablecoins in cold storage than rely entirely on foreign banks and unpredictable policies.

WHAT'S HAPPENING AROUND THE WORLD

In 2024, *El Salvador made headlines* by being the first country to adopt Bitcoin as legal tender. But what shocked the world more was when it began buying Bitcoin for its national treasury. Skeptics mocked it. But when Bitcoin prices rebounded, El Salvador's holdings doubled—and its economy became a case study in long-term digital strategy.

Then came **Venezuela, Nigeria, Ukraine**, and others—countries with unstable currencies, banking restrictions, or limited access to global capital.

They turned to crypto not as a rebellion, but as a solution.

By 2026, rumors began surfacing that even developed nations—quietly, unofficially—were experimenting with holding small portions of national reserves in crypto as a hedge.

It wasn't a revolution overnight. It was a shift in mindset.

INDIA'S SILENT AWAKENING

India has always had a complex relationship with crypto. On one hand, it houses one of the largest populations of crypto users in the world. On the other, its policy stance has been cautious, at times skeptical.

But after the events of 2025—the inflation spike, global devaluation, and capital flight—India began to reconsider its long-term strategy.

By 2030, several Indian states had launched pilot programs to test crypto reserves at a micro level—holding small percentages of surplus budgets in Bitcoin or stablecoins to test resilience, speed, and returns.

Banks started tokenizing their assets. Nationalized banks began offering custody services for crypto. And whispers began to circulate within RBI circles: Should we begin to allocate 1% to Bitcoin? Just as a hedge?

After all, gold has served as a hedge for decades.

Why not digital gold?

WHAT MAKES THIS SHIFT SO PROFOUND?

This shift from central bank reserves to crypto isn't just a financial story. It's a paradigm shift.

It represents a change in how we define value, trust, and control.

- Central banks are about monopoly over money.
- Crypto is about money without monopoly.
- Central reserves are about external dependence.
- Crypto reserves are about internal sovereignty.

For countries like India, which balance modern finance with traditional values, the move toward decentralized reserves is not just about staying trendy—it's about survival, independence, and future-proofing.

As the world becomes more digitized, and financial systems become more programmable, every country will need to decide:

Do we continue to store our safety in institutions that can fail? Or in code that cannot lie?

This transition won't happen overnight. But it has already started.

India doesn't need to abandon the rupee. It doesn't need to replace gold. But it can evolve its reserve strategy—diversifying into digital, borderless, incorruptible assets that give it greater control, flexibility, and strength in a world no longer run on paper promises.

Tomorrow's financial wars won't be fought with tanks or sanctions—but with liquidity, transparency, and algorithmic trust.

Central banks may still sit at the top of the pyramid. But that pyramid is flattening. And at the base, crypto reserves are rising.

FROM LEGACY TO LEDGER

In 1991, India opened its economy to the world. In the decades since, it has become a tech giant, a digital economy leader, and a global force.

Now, in this new era, the next bold step awaits:
redefining what we hold, how we hold it, and why.

The shift from central banks to crypto reserves isn't just economic—it's existential.

It's about control. It's about resilience.

But above all, it's about trust.

And as more Indians begin to trust math over ministries, code over committees, and ledgers over letters, one thing becomes clear:

The future of reserves is not in vaults. It's on the blockchain.

2035: HOW BITCOIN IS USED IN INDIA TODAY

Hyderabad, 2035,

It's a warm evening in Jubilee Hills. Neon lights hum softly above cafés, coworking hubs, and AI-run dosa stalls. Inside a popular startup lounge, 18-year-old Kavya is finishing a meeting with her DAO. She receives her monthly stipend in Bitcoin, instantly, with zero fees, directly into her self-custody wallet.

She doesn't even blink—because this is normal now.

Welcome to India, 2035.

A country that once questioned the legitimacy of Bitcoin now uses it in ways no one in 2020 could've imagined. From bustling metros to remote Ladakhi villages, Bitcoin has woven itself into India's economic, cultural, and technological fabric—not as a replacement for the rupee, but as a parallel system of value, trust, and independence.

This isn't science fiction.

This is the logical evolution of a nation that adapted faster than anyone expected. And it all started with a need for control in a world spinning too fast.

THE BITCOIN SHIFT: FROM OBSCURITY TO UTILITY

Back in 2023, most Indians thought of Bitcoin as a risky investment, a speculative game for techies and early adopters. Wallets were complicated. Regulation was confusing. Volatility scared people.

But slowly, piece by piece, that changed.

By the late 2020s, two things became undeniable:

The rupee was weakening. Inflation, rising import costs, and global economic shifts made saving in fiat harder.

Bitcoin was surviving everything. Bans, bear markets, media attacks—it just kept running. Block by block, it proved it didn't need permission to exist.

People started noticing. First the tech-savvy. Then freelancers. Then traders. Then the everyday Indian.

By 2030, after the Great Currency Devaluation of 2025 and the widespread adoption of digital assets globally, India began to lean into Bitcoin—not with fear, but with curiosity.

The government didn't outlaw it. Instead, it accepted that Bitcoin wasn't going anywhere. It was better to regulate, integrate, and observe than to resist.

That decision turned India into one of the fastest-growing crypto-integrated economies in the world.

So, How Do Indians Use Bitcoin in 2035?

Not just technically, but through real, lived experience

PAYMENTS WITHOUT PERMISSION

In 2035, Bitcoin is one of the most common forms of cross-border payment in India.

Freelancers across Bengaluru, Jaipur, and Kolkata receive salaries in Bitcoin from international clients in minutes—no PayPal limits, no 3-day bank delays, no hidden fees.

A carpenter in Kerala now accepts small satoshi payments from NRIs paying for custom work. A wedding planner in Udaipur books high-end NRI events and gets paid in BTC—taxed and declared, but fast, secure, and stored safely.

Even chaiwalas and kirana store owners in urban areas offer Bitcoin Lightning Network options for small transactions. The new UPI 3.0 has integrated a Bitcoin layer, making Bitcoin just as usable as rupees—except it's borderless and fully controlled by the user.

SMART SAVINGS WITH HARD MONEY

Sonal, a schoolteacher in Pune, no longer keeps all her savings in her bank's fixed deposits. Every month, she auto-converts 20% of her income into Bitcoin using a digital rupee-to-BTC bridge built into her salary app.
She's not doing this to "get rich." She's doing it because she doesn't trust fiat to protect her future anymore.

Bitcoin has become India's new digital locker—the modern equivalent of storing gold in the cupboard. But unlike gold, it can't be stolen. It can't be forged. It can't be taxed into worthlessness through inflation.

And it's accessible 24/7—on the train, in the village, on the mountain.

COLLATERAL AND CREDIT

Banks in 2035 don't just ask for land records or income statements. They also accept Bitcoin as collateral.

A farmer in Gujarat used his 0.3 BTC savings as security for a low-interest loan to upgrade his irrigation system. A college student in Chennai staked her BTC to borrow USDC for tuition payments, repaid over time via smart contracts.

No paperwork. No begging. No delays.
Bitcoin-backed lending has opened credit to millions who were previously excluded.

Decentralized finance (DeFi) platforms regulated in India offer fully automated, government-compliant lending systems—with transparency, fairness, and open access.

GOVERNMENT ADOPTION & SOVEREIGN INTEGRATION

This might be the most shocking shift of all.
In 2035, several Indian states now hold Bitcoin in treasury reserves. Not as speculation—but as a hedge. A security net against global fiat volatility.

During global liquidity crises or dollar instability, these Bitcoin reserves help states protect subsidies, maintain essential imports, and even attract foreign investment.
Some municipalities issue Bitcoin bonds, allowing Indian citizens to invest directly in local development projects—railways, green tech, healthcare—earning interest paid in BTC.

This has built direct trust between citizens and government—a bond stronger than any rupee ever offered.

DIGITAL IDENTITY AND OWNERSHIP

In the post-Aadhaar evolution, many Indians now have Bitcoin-linked decentralized IDs—used for secure authentication, voting in DAOs, and managing personal data.

Artists mint music, writers mint books, students mint certificates—all hashed and verified using Bitcoin's immutable layer.

Ownership has become frictionless and permanent. You don't "prove" you own something anymore. You just show your Bitcoin-backed digital signature.

THE CULTURAL SHIFT: MORE THAN JUST TECH

But the biggest shift is not financial. It's psychological.
India is a country that once bowed to bureaucracy and waited for approval. Bitcoin changed that. It gave people, especially the youth, something powerful but invisible—a sense of control.

You don't need a banker's nod to own BTC. You don't need to stand in line. You don't need a permission slip to move your wealth, grow your savings, or access the global economy.

This quiet empowerment has ignited a generation of builders, savers, creators, and investors who no longer ask,
"Can I?"
They ask,
"How much?" "When?" "Why not now?"

BITCOIN IS NOT JUST USED—IT'S LIVED

By 2035, Bitcoin is no longer an "*investment trend*" in India.

It's part of the financial bloodstream. A tool for payments. A vault for savings. A bridge to opportunity. A firewall against inflation. A gateway to global wealth.

Most importantly, it's owned directly—by the people. No bank can freeze it. No politician can print it. No border can block it.

Aayush, a 12-year-old from Assam, just received a scholarship in Bitcoin. Kavya, running her DAO, built an app in Hindi to help her village use Lightning payments. Ramesh, once skeptical, now pays rent to his tenant in BTC.

The old system still exists—but it now shares space with something sharper, faster, fairer.

In India, 2035, Bitcoin is not the future.

It's the present.
And it's not just being used—it's being trusted.

INDIA 2035: BITCOIN IN ACTION – REAL STORIES FROM A TRANSFORMED NATION

The shift wasn't just in apps or headlines. It was in everyday life. From metros to mandis, Bitcoin had seeped into the cracks of India's economy—not as a buzzword, but as a backbone.

Here's how it looks on the ground:

MUMBAI STOCK EXCHANGE – NOW TOKENIZED ON BLOCKCHAIN

The iconic Dalal Street still stands, but what happens inside is unrecognizable from a decade ago. Stockbrokers no longer deal in rupees alone. Bitcoin, Ethereum, and tokenized shares of Indian corporations are traded 24/7 on blockchain rails. Settlement time? Seconds. Cross-border participation? Instant. It's a global, decentralized market with Indian efficiency and global liquidity.

CHENNAI'S IT HUBS – SALARIES PAID IN CRYPTO

Walk into any tech park in Tidel Park or OMR Road, and you'll find coders not just collecting rupee salaries—but receiving 20% to 40% of their income in Bitcoin or stablecoins. It's not just about returns. It's about sovereignty. No more waiting for international transfers or converting foreign pay through banks. The best minds now get paid in assets that grow, not just cash that erodes.

KOLKATA'S ART & FILM SCENE - NFTS & GLOBAL ROYALTIES

Tollywood and Bollywood have both embraced the crypto wave. Musicians, digital artists, and indie filmmakers now mint their creations as NFTs, earning Bitcoin royalties from fans in London, Tokyo, and New York. No middlemen. No delayed payments. Just global reach and direct, programmable income.

A SMALL VILLAGE IN MAHARASHTRA - BLOCKCHAIN-POWERED FARMING

In a remote region near Satara, farmers use smart contracts on blockchain to sell produce directly to urban buyers. The payment—often in Bitcoin or stablecoins—is automatic once delivery is confirmed via IoT-linked supply chains. No exploitation. No late payments. No corrupt intermediaries. Just clean, instant, fair trade.

DELHI'S PARLIAMENT - BITCOIN IN TRADE & TREASURY STRATEGY

Behind the red sandstone walls of India's Parliament, things have changed too. Bitcoin is now a strategic reserve—a small but symbolic part of India's international trade arsenal. With Bitcoin, India pays for global energy contracts, secures digital trade pacts, and hedges against dollar volatility. Regulatory frameworks are no longer about "should we allow Bitcoin?"—they're about how to lead with it.

WILL BITCOIN FULLY REPLACE GOLD?

Even in 2035, gold hasn't vanished. It still gleams at weddings, sits in lockers, and fills temple donation boxes. It's part of our emotion, our tradition, our culture. Central banks still hold it. Brides still wear it. Families still cherish it.

But the world has evolved.

Where gold was once the only trustworthy store of value, Bitcoin has emerged as its digital twin—and for many, its successor.

For the younger generation, Bitcoin is gold—but lighter, smarter, and immune to inflation. It doesn't sit in vaults. It moves through wallets. It's divisible, programmable, and secure. It's as much a part of a millennial's financial plan as gold was to their grandparents.

For businesses and investors, Bitcoin is not a gamble—it's a shield. Against inflation. Against manipulation. Against monetary instability. It's a liquid, global, incorruptible asset.

And for governments?

Bitcoin is leverage.

It's financial neutrality.

It's a seat at the new global table, where power is no longer just about armies and oil—but about who owns digital value that no central bank can inflate.

The Question Has Changed

Back in 2020, people used to ask,

"Is Bitcoin real?"

"Is it legal?"
"Is it safe?"

In 2035, those questions sound almost naive.

Now the question is:

Will you adapt to this new era?

Or will you wait, hoping the old system saves you—even as it quietly fades away?

This is India's Bitcoin Moment.

It's not about replacing tradition. It's about upgrading it.

It's not about rejecting the rupee. It's about balancing it.

It's not about waiting for the future. It's about owning it.

One block at a time.
One satoshi at a time.
One bold choice at a time.

India has already moved.

The only question left is:

Have you?

Mnemonic to Remember Bitcoin's Strengths

S.P.I.C.E

Scarce

Portable

Immune to inflation

Censorship-resistant

Easy to verify

*****

"DeFi is not about replacing banks with new banks—it's about removing the need for banks altogether."

©Andreas M. Antonopoulos

CHAPTER THREE

THE RISE OF DEFI – A WORLD WITHOUT BANKS?

"What we're building with DeFi isn't just a better bank – it's a world where you don't need one."

-----***Andreas M. Antonopoulos*** *(Bitcoin and blockchain educator)*

Mumbai, 2035,

Pankaj stood on his balcony, sipping chai as the sun lit up the skyline of Lower Parel. He checked his phone—not to scroll through social media, but to review his investments, savings, and loan repayments. Except none of this involved a bank.

No bank branches. No paperwork. No waiting for approvals.

Pankaj was managing everything through a DeFi protocol—an ecosystem of decentralized finance that had, over the past decade, rewritten the rules of money. With just a smartphone and an internet connection, he was earning interest, lending capital, insuring digital assets, and managing risk without stepping into a bank even once.

This wasn't a futuristic fantasy anymore. This was the new normal.

And for millions across India and the world, DeFi—Decentralized Finance—had become more than a buzzword. It was a quiet, unstoppable revolution.

THE OLD BANKING SYSTEM: A SLOW, EXPENSIVE MONOPOLY

For centuries, banks were the undisputed gatekeepers of money. They controlled who could open an account, who was "eligible" for a loan, and who could send or receive money—especially across borders. They decided your financial worth, often with zero transparency. And they made sure you paid for the privilege at every step.
If you wanted access to the financial system, there was no negotiation. You had to go through a bank.

WHAT DID THAT LOOK LIKE?

- **High fees:** Transfer charges. Withdrawal charges. "Maintenance" charges. Every click had a cost.

- **Slow service:** Sending money abroad? Expect 3–5 working days, tons of paperwork, and hidden charges.

- **Limited access:** Over **1.7** billion people globally—millions in India alone—had no bank account. No access to loans. No formal savings.
- **Government control:** At any moment, your bank account could be frozen. Transactions blocked. Permissions denied.

Banks didn't just hold money. They controlled lives.
And for decades, we accepted it—because we had no choice.
Until something changed.

Then Came Blockchain. Then Came DeFi.

When blockchain emerged, it promised transparency.

When Bitcoin was born, it offered independence.

But when DeFi (Decentralized Finance) entered the scene—it offered freedom, at scale.

Suddenly, you didn't need to stand in line.

You didn't need a banker's signature.
You didn't need anyone's permission.

You just needed a phone.
An internet connection.
And a wallet you controlled.

DeFi Didn't Upgrade Banking – It Replaced the Blueprint

Traditional banks are like old castles — strong but slow, guarded by gatekeepers, and built on trust in institutions. DeFi is like a digital network of automated portals — fast, borderless, and built on code. One doesn't improve the other. It rewrites the rules entirely.

DeFi didn't upgrade the old banking system. It bypassed it entirely.

- ❖ Want to earn interest? Deposit into a smart contract and watch your assets grow in real time.
- ❖ Need a loan? Lock your crypto as collateral and borrow instantly—no credit score required.
- ❖ Sending money abroad? Just send. It's settled in seconds, not days.

No branches. No bureaucracy. No middlemen.

And best of all?

You're in charge.

FROM BANKS TO BLOCKCHAIN: WHAT IS DEFI, REALLY?

DeFi is short for *Decentralized Finance*. It's an alternative financial system built not on bank buildings or government policies, but on blockchain networks, mostly Ethereum (and now many others).

Instead of relying on intermediaries like banks, brokers, and regulators, DeFi uses smart contracts—self-executing code that runs exactly as written.

These contracts can handle:

- ❖ Lending & borrowing
- ❖ Trading assets
- ❖ Earning interest
- ❖ Insurance
- ❖ Stablecoins and payments

All without middlemen.

No gatekeepers.

No KYC delays.

No service fees draining your balance.

It's like replacing the entire banking system with open-source software—global, programmable, and unstoppable.

HOW DEFI IS TRANSFORMING INDIA'S FINANCIAL FUTURE

The bankless revolution has gone local—and it's changing everything.

In a country like India, where bureaucratic banking, delayed approvals, and financial exclusion have been the norm for decades, DeFi has not just entered the chat—it's rewriting the script.

No more standing in line.

No more paperwork.

No more asking for permission.

Instead, with just a smartphone, millions of Indians are accessing instant loans, borderless payments, transparent investments, and true financial freedom.

<u>HERE'S WHAT IT LOOKS LIKE ON THE GROUND:</u>

RURAL INDIA - FARMERS REAP FINANCIAL FREEDOM WITH DEFI LOANS

Across Maharashtra, Tamil Nadu, and parts of Bihar, farmers are no longer dependent on local moneylenders or uncooperative banks.

They now borrow stablecoins backed by real-world assets using blockchain-based lending protocols.

No collateral required. No bias. No delays.

- Loan approvals in seconds.
- Smart contracts ensure automatic repayments after harvest
- No corruption, no middlemen, no exploitation

For the first time, a small farmer in India can access global capital—as easily as opening a WhatsApp message.

IN TRADITIONAL FINANCE

Interest = Principal x Rate x Time

(And most of it goes to the bank.)

IN DEFI

Smart Contract + Liquidity Pool = Direct Interest to You

Platforms like **Aave** or **Compound** allow users to deposit stablecoins and **earn real-time interest**. No branches. No paperwork.

EXAMPLE

A user deposits 1,000 USDC into Compound. At 5% APY, they watch their balance grow—minute by minute—visible on-chain, with full control and transparency.

BENGALURU – FREELANCERS & TECH WORKERS PAID IN CRYPTO

The IT capital of India has gone global—literally.

Developers, designers, coders, and digital consultants now receive their salaries in USDC and Bitcoin directly into their wallets.

- No PayPal delay
- No conversion losses
- No need for a bank at all

And most of all, no one is taking a cut of their hard-earned money.

For India's digital workforce, DeFi isn't an option—it's a financial upgrade.

DELHI – WOMEN ENTREPRENEURS BREAK THE SYSTEM, NOT THEMSELVES

In the narrow lanes of Chandni Chowk and the modern co-working spaces of Connaught Place, women-led businesses are rising—with zero dependence on traditional banks.

Through DeFi microloan platforms, women are now:

- Accessing funding without collateral
- Raising capital without discrimination
- Paying back loans through automated smart contracts

Banks that once asked for husbands' signatures or family land records are now irrelevant.
The code doesn't care who you are—it only cares if the math works.

MUMBAI - THE STOCK MARKET GOES ON-CHAIN

Dalal Street has changed forever.

Stocks, real estate, gold, and bonds are now tokenized and fractionalized—traded on blockchain 24/7, with no brokers, no paperwork, and no minimum capital.

A teenager with ₹100 can now invest in:

- A fraction of a Mumbai apartment
- Shares of Reliance tokenized on Ethereum
- Gold-backed tokens with instant liquidity

This isn't just innovation. It's access, finally made real.

WHY THE WORLD TURNED TO DEFI

Traditional banking was built for a world of paper, signatures, and 9-to-5 service hours. But people now live in a world that's 24/7, mobile-first, and borderless.

Banks were slow to adapt—and in many places, corrupt or inaccessible.

In India alone:

- Millions still don't have access to formal credit.
- Rural citizens face long waits and paperwork just to open an account.
- Small businesses are often denied loans for arbitrary reasons.

- ❖ Bank servers crash during peak hours.

And even for those with access, trust is thin. High fees. Poor service. No transparency.

DeFi flipped the script.

It said:

"What if you could borrow without begging?"
"What if your money earned more while you sleep?"
"What if you controlled your finances—without trusting anyone?"

It wasn't just about building new systems.

It was about reclaiming control.

HOW DEFI WORKS – FOR THE COMMON INDIAN

Let's say Priti, a 26-year-old graphic designer in Pune, wants to:

- ❖ Earn interest on her savings.
- ❖ Get a small loan for a laptop upgrade.
- ❖ Invest safely in USD-pegged stablecoins

In 2019, she'd go to a bank, wait in line, fill a form, and hope to qualify. She might be rejected just because her job is "freelance."

In 2035, Priti logs into a DeFi app on her phone. It connects to her crypto wallet. She deposits ₹50,000 worth of stablecoins.
Immediately:
She starts earning 8–10% APY—far higher than her old savings account.

She can borrow against her savings in minutes—with no credit score needed.

Her data stays private. Her money stays with her.
It's financial inclusion at code speed.

And she's not alone. From Uber drivers in Hyderabad to artisans in Jaipur, millions now access capital directly through DeFi—no banker, no manager, no waiting room.

LOANS WITHOUT A BANKER'S APPROVAL

Collateral (in ETH) + Smart Contract Logic = Instant Loan (in USDC or DAI)

In CeFi (Centralized Finance): You apply. Wait. Get judged. In DeFi: You **lock your crypto** and **borrow instantly**. No KYC. No credit score.

EXAMPLE

Ravi locks 2 ETH (worth ₹4,00,000) into Aave. He instantly borrows ₹2,00,000 in stablecoins. If the ETH price drops below a safety threshold, the smart contract liquidates automatically—no humans needed.

DAOS: THE NEW DIGITAL CREDIT SOCIETIES

In rural India, cooperative banks and credit societies have long served small communities. But they're limited by scale and prone to local politics.

Now, enter DAOs—Decentralized Autonomous Organizations.

Imagine a village in Tamil Nadu creating a smart contract-based fund where farmers pool savings and borrow transparently, governed by collective votes. No corruption. No bias. No hidden terms.

DAOs have become the digital version of credit societies—global, transparent, and programmable.

Even local governments are beginning to support "Community DAOs" for self-managed rural finance, grants, and local development

THE FLIP SIDE: IS DEFI RISK-FREE?

Absolutely not.

Like any powerful tool, DeFi has its risks:

- Smart contracts can be buggy or hacked.
- Tokens can be volatile.
- Scams and rug pull still exist.
- If you lose your private keys, you lose your funds—no helpline will help you.

But unlike traditional finance, the rules are visible. The risks are known. And DeFi users are becoming more educated, cautious, and empowered.

It’s open risk, not hidden manipulation.

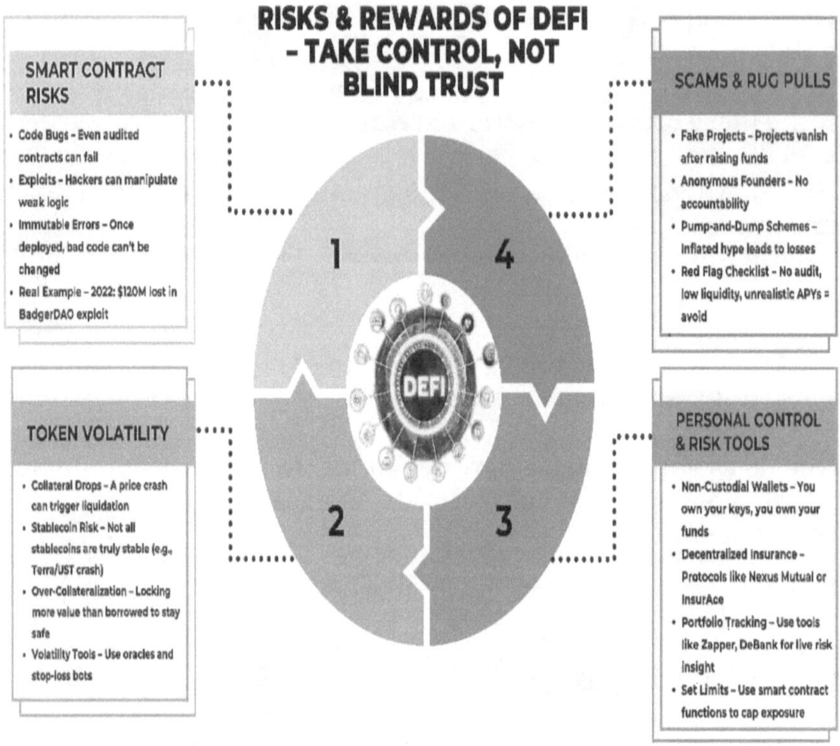

THE IMPACT ON BANKS: ADAPT OR DIE

Banks laughed at DeFi. Then they tried to regulate it. Now they’re racing to copy it.

In 2035:

❖ India’s largest public banks offer DeFi-like services—but still require identity verification.

❖ New digital banks run entirely on blockchain protocols, with RBI oversight.

- The RBI has launched its own DeFi sandbox to explore lending, insurance, and stablecoin tools built on public blockchains.

But the truth is clear:

DeFi didn't just disrupt banking. It redefined the purpose of a bank.

Banks are no longer gatekeepers. They're becoming service providers in an open system. Either they innovate—or they become irrelevant.

THE RBI'S RESPONSE: ENTER THE DIGITAL RUPEE (CBDC)

The Reserve Bank of India didn't sit still. In response to DeFi's rise, it launched the Digital Rupee (CBDC)—a blockchain-powered currency issued by the government.

- Faster payments
- Programmable tax collection
- Institutional legitimacy

But there's a catch.

- It's digital—but not decentralized.
- It's programmable—but still controlled.
- It's official—but still vulnerable to inflation.

So, the question Indians are now asking is:

"Why choose the Digital Rupee, when DeFi already gives me more freedom?"

WHY INDIA IS LEADING THE DEFI WAVE

India's mix of:

- A massive digital user base
- Deep-rooted mistrust of bureaucracy
- A culture of savings and micro-entrepreneurship
- World-class tech talent

...has made it the perfect ground for DeFi to explode.

Today, India is not just using DeFi. It is building it.

Thousands of Indian developers contribute to global DeFi protocols. New unicorns are born from Tier-2 cities. Indian DAOs fund education, green energy, and local farming innovations.

For the world, DeFi is a trend.

For India, it's infrastructure.

A WORLD WITHOUT BANKS

In 2035, kids in India are growing up using DeFi apps instead of piggy banks.

Farmers in Madhya Pradesh secure crop insurance through smart contracts.
A college student in Bengaluru earns yield on her Bitcoin without trusting any financial advisor.

An artist in Shillong sells music NFTs and gets paid instantly in stablecoins—no label, no bank, no delay.

This is not theory. This is reality.

The old financial empire, once unquestioned, is now being replaced by a permissionless economy that rewards transparency, speed, and fairness.

DeFi has exposed a truth we always knew but never challenged: The traditional banking system wasn't slow and expensive by accident—it was slow and expensive by design.

The banking system had centuries to fix its flaws.
But instead of becoming more inclusive, it became more exclusive.

Instead of empowering people, it trained them to ask for permission.

Instead of innovating, it clung to power.

And now, the people have found an alternative.

Not a better bank.

A world without banks.

DeFi isn't just a product.
It's a philosophy.

It's the belief that you don't need a middleman to be free.
And it all started the moment someone asked:

"What if we just built a system where banks weren't necessary at all?"

That system is here. It's growing. It's borderless.
And it's not coming for banks.

It's replacing them.

No more waiting in line. No more asking for approval. No more hidden fees.

This is finance, reimagined.

Welcome to DeFi—the world where you are the bank.

WILL DEFI COMPLETELY REPLACE BANKS?

Maybe not entirely. Banks still offer important trust layers for some use cases. They still serve the offline population and offer regulatory stability.

DeFi didn't come to fix banks.
It came to replace their function with better technology, fairer systems, and global access.

India, once underserved by banks, is now leading the charge. From farmers to freelancers, women to wealth managers, students to state governments—the DeFi revolution is already here.

And the question isn't whether it will succeed.

It already has.

The only question is:

Will you join, or will you be left behind?

Because in 2035, there are two types of people:

Those still asking for permission.
And those who just connect their wallet—and go.

But what's clear is this:

You no longer need a bank to be financially free.
You just need a wallet, a protocol, and a little courage.

The question is no longer "*Can DeFi work?*"

It's "*Can you afford to ignore it?*"

In the past, people asked banks for permission.

In the DeFi future, you ask no one.

You transact, you borrow, you earn, you build—freely.

And in a world that once said, “Trust us, we’re the bank,”

DeFi replies:

“Trust the code.”

*****

"At first they ignore Bitcoin, then they laugh at it, then they fight it–and then, it becomes inevitable."

©Andreas M. Antonopoulos (Bitcoin advocate, Author of The Internet of Money)

CHAPTER FOUR

THE GLOBAL ADOPTION CURVE: FROM DOUBT TO DECENTRALIZED REVOLUTION

"Bitcoin is a hedge against the whole system. As more people wake up to that, the adoption will be unstoppable."
------- ***Chamath Palihapitiya*** *(Venture capitalist)*

The year is 2035,

And what started as a whisper in forums, a curiosity for nerds, and a rebellion against Wall Street... has now become a global movement.

Bitcoin, once laughed at by bankers and dismissed by economists, is now being held by governments, billionaires, farmers, and teenagers alike.

DeFi, once considered risky and dangerous, is now powering entire economies, issuing real loans, and handling trillions in value—without a single bank involved.

But this didn't happen overnight.
It happened in phases—like every world-changing technology.
And now, we're watching the global adoption curve of crypto and DeFi unfold in real time.

This is the story of how the world didn't just accept decentralized finance...
It needed it.

STAGE 1: THE NERD PHASE (2009–2015)

Every revolution starts with a small group of people that everyone else ignores.

For Bitcoin, it was developers, cypherpunks, and idealists—people who questioned the central banking system after the 2008 financial collapse.

They weren't in it for profit.

They were in it for *freedom.*

This phase was full of:

- Mining BTC on laptops
- Long philosophical debates on Reddit
- Pure tech innovation, with no marketing

To the rest of the world, they looked crazy.

But they were building the foundation of a financial system that needed no permission to exist.

STAGE 2: THE EARLY ADOPTER PHASE (2016–2020)

This is when the outside world started paying attention. Bitcoin crossed $1,000. Then $10,000.

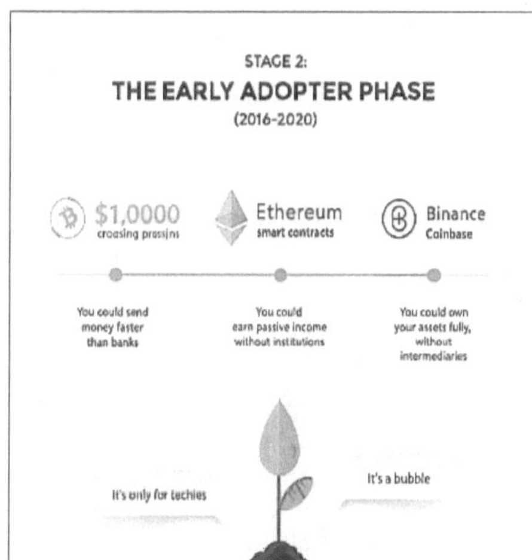

Ethereum introduced smart contracts.

Exchanges like Binance and Coinbase exploded.

People began to realize:
You could send money faster than banks.

You could earn passive income without institutions.

You could own your assets fully, without intermediaries
Still, it was early.
Most people were skeptical.

They said, "*It's a bubble.*"
They said, "*It's only for techies.*"

But beneath the surface, the seed had been planted.

STAGE 3: THE INFRASTRUCTURE BOOM (2021–2025)

This was the growth spurt.

New blockchains (Solana, Avalanche, Polygon) came up. DeFi protocols like Aave, Uniswap, and Compound changed the game.

Stablecoins like USDC and USDT became the default for cross-border money.

NFTs unlocked digital ownership.

Then came the Great Currency Devaluation of 2025.

Governments printed too much money.
Inflation soared.

People lost trust in fiat.

And suddenly, *DeFi wasn't a toy—it was a necessity.*

Countries like Argentina, Nigeria, Turkey, and Venezuela saw mass adoption as people rushed to protect their wealth.

In India, crypto usage quietly passed 200 million users.

This was no longer about speculation.

It was about survival.

STAGE 4: INSTITUTIONAL ENTRY (2026–2030)

This is when the big players walked in.

Asset managers began holding Bitcoin on their balance sheets

Banks started offering DeFi-based savings and loans

Countries added BTC to their national reserves.

ETFs and tokenized securities went mainstream
Even skeptics began to hedge their doubts with a little crypto in their portfolios.

This was the *"too big to ignore"* phase.

And while the old guard tried to regulate or compete, the smart ones started building on-chain banking infrastructure.

STAGE 5: THE EVERYDAY PHASE (2030–2035)

And now, here we are. In 2035, crypto is no longer something you "invest" in. It's something you use.
Every day.

People get paid in stablecoins.

Real estate is bought with tokenized assets

Government services run on smart contracts

Small businesses use DeFi for working capital

Education is certified on blockchain

Healthcare records are stored in encrypted wallets

Cross-border trade runs on decentralized ledgers

This isn't hype. It's infrastructure.

From Manali to Mumbai, Lagos to London, people are finally in control of their money, identity, and future.

And guess what?
Most of them never even say the word "crypto."
They just use it—because it works better.

But Adoption Isn't Equal Everywhere (Yet)

Even in 2035, the adoption curve is still uneven.

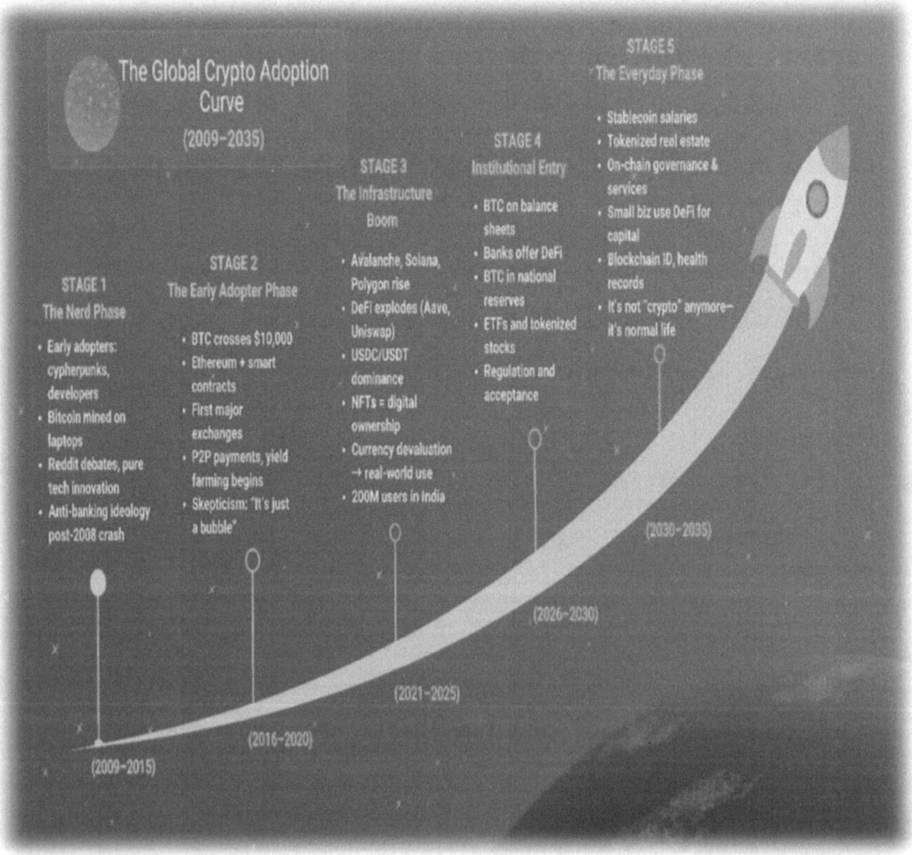

GLOBAL SOUTH: THE LEADERS

Countries with failing currencies and corrupt banks were the first to jump in.
Why? Because they needed financial independence the most.

- In Africa, farmers use DeFi to get crop insurance and sell goods directly.
- In Latin America, stablecoins are more trusted than local currencies.
- In South Asia, freelancers get paid globally via crypto wallets.
- These regions skipped the bank-based model and jumped straight into bankless finance.

THE WEST: PLAYING CATCH UP

Ironically, wealthier countries were slower.
Their systems worked—until they didn't.

When inflation hit and traditional banks collapsed, people started waking up.

Now, Americans and Europeans are using DeFi more, not for survival—but for better returns, lower fees, and more control.

THE REAL STORY OF BITCOIN ADOPTION

A decade ago, Bitcoin was a curiosity—a strange idea floating around in forums, discussed by cryptographers, libertarians, and a handful of tech dreamers. It was labelled a "fad," a "scam," even "magic internet money." Most people ignored it. Governments dismissed it. Banks laughed at it.

But the world changed.

And so did Bitcoin.

Today, entire nations are debating its future. Some are regulating it. Others are embracing it completely. From street vendors in Lagos to billion-dollar hedge funds in New York, from Himalayan freelancers to Latin American presidents—Bitcoin has gone global.

But why is this happening now?

And who's really driving this revolution?

THE FIRST-MOVERS: COUNTRIES THAT BET BIG ON BITCOIN

While many nations still sit on the fence, a few have moved boldly. Not with hesitation, but with conviction. These countries didn't just regulate Bitcoin—they integrated it into their national strategy. Some out of necessity. Others out of vision.

EL SALVADOR: THE FIRST BITCOIN NATION

In 2021, a moment in history was made. El Salvador became the first country in the world to declare Bitcoin legal tender. Spearheaded by the young and daring President Nayib Bukele, the move wasn't just symbolic. It was a direct challenge to the global financial order.

WHY DID THEY DO IT?

Because 70% of El Salvador's population had no access to banks.
Because remittances made up more than 20% of its GDP—and companies like Western Union were charging massive fees.
Because they saw Bitcoin not as a threat, but as an opportunity to leapfrog into the future.

KEY IMPACTS:

Chivo Wallet & Free Bitcoin

The government launched a national crypto wallet and gave every citizen $30 worth of Bitcoin to get started. Overnight, the country went from 0 to over 3 million Bitcoin users.

Bitcoin ATMs Everywhere

From malls to markets, Bitcoin ATMs started appearing—turning El Salvador into the world's first live crypto laboratory.

Tourism & Investment Surge

Crypto investors and entrepreneurs flocked to El Salvador, sparking a wave of tech startups and global attention.

Adoption hasn't been smooth. Many citizens still prefer cash. Price volatility has caused concern. And international institutions weren't thrilled. But the experiment is ongoing—and the world is watching. El Salvador planted a flag in uncharted territory. And history will remember it.

NIGERIA: CRYPTO IN THE FACE OF CHAOS

Unlike El Salvador, Nigeria didn't officially adopt Bitcoin. The people did.

With a struggling currency (the Naira), soaring inflation, limited banking infrastructure, and strict government controls—Nigerians turned to Bitcoin out of pure necessity. It wasn't about ideology. It was about survival.

And what happened next shocked the world.

KEY DRIVERS OF NIGERIA'S CRYPTO BOOM

Peer-to-Peer (P2P) Trading

When the government restricted crypto transactions through banks, Nigerians simply moved to P2P platforms. Today, Nigeria leads the world in P2P Bitcoin trading volume.

A Store of Value Against Inflation

As prices soared and savings lost value, Bitcoin became a financial shield. For many Nigerians, it was the only stable place to park their money.

Youth-Led Digital Uprising

With one of the youngest populations on Earth and widespread mobile usage, Nigeria's digital-native generation embraced crypto faster than regulators could react.

Result?

Bitcoin adoption exploded—despite bans, media fear, and state opposition.
Nigerians didn't ask for permission.
They opted out.

BEYOND BORDERS: THE GLOBAL MOMENTUM

These two countries are just the beginning.
Bitcoin is spreading across the globe like a digital wildfire—and every region is embracing it in its own way.

LATIN AMERICA

Countries like **Argentina** and **Venezuela** have turned to Bitcoin as local currencies collapse. Inflation rates above 50% have made crypto the default store of value for citizens who no longer trust their governments.

UNITED STATES

Major financial institutions, from BlackRock to JP Morgan, now hold and trade Bitcoin. Bitcoin ETFs have gone live. Pension funds are allocating small percentages to crypto. The narrative has shifted from "scam" to "strategic hedge.

UKRAINE

During the 2022 conflict, crypto donations kept the Ukrainian economy alive. Citizens used Bitcoin and stablecoins to escape capital controls and move money across borders when banks couldn't.

INDIA

While India hasn't formally adopted Bitcoin as legal tender, the people are way ahead. With over **200 million crypto users**, India is one of the largest crypto markets in the world. Freelancers, investors, and small businesses increasingly use Bitcoin and DeFi tools to earn, save, and transact globally.

WHY NOW? WHY IS THE WORLD ADOPTING BITCOIN?

Across the globe—from the mighty U.S. dollar to the fragile Turkish lira—trust in traditional currencies is fading. Central banks, in a desperate attempt to keep systems afloat, are printing trillions out of thin air. And with every new note printed, people feel their purchasing power quietly slipping away. Inflation is no longer an abstract threat—its dinner plates costing more, savings losing value, and the sense of security vanishing. In this new world, people are beginning to search for something different. Something that doesn't lie. Something that can't be manipulated.

And then, there's Bitcoin.

For the digital generation—the ones who grew up on the internet, streaming ideas at light speed—the old financial system doesn't hold the same authority it once did. They don't trust banks the way their parents did. They trust code. They trust algorithms. They trust open systems built on transparency and rules, not backroom deals. To them, a decentralized currency like Bitcoin feels more natural than a cheque book or a savings account. It's not just money—it's philosophy coded into reality.

But the real revolution is happening quietly in places where banks never reached. Over 1.7 billion people around the world live without access to basic financial services. No accounts. No credit. No banks. Yet most of them have a smartphone in their hand. And that's where Bitcoin changes everything. With just an internet connection and a digital wallet, a farmer in rural India or a vendor in Nigeria can now participate in global finance—without needing anyone's permission. No branches. No paperwork. Just freedom.

In a time when institutions are tightening their grip—watching, tracking, and sometimes freezing accounts at will—Bitcoin offers something rare: sovereignty. It gives people the power to own their wealth completely. No middlemen. No gatekeepers. No one to censor or seize. "Your keys, your coins"—it's more than a slogan. It's a promise of financial autonomy in a world increasingly built on control.

This isn't just a currency shift. It's a trust shift.

WHERE IS THIS HEADED?

The adoption curve isn't slowing down—it's accelerating.
We're moving from early adopters to global integration.

- Bitcoin on national balance sheets
- Salaries paid in BTC and stablecoins
- Cross-border trade settled in crypto
- Governments launching Bitcoin bonds
- Institutions offering crypto-native services

In the next decade, Bitcoin won't just be part of the financial system—it will be the foundation of a parallel, borderless, permissionless financial world.

The Revolution Is Not Coming. It's Here.

Bitcoin is no longer just a niche experiment whispered about on internet forums. It has transformed—from a digital joke passed around as memes to a serious global movement reshaping how we think about money.
What began as a rebel asset outside the system... is now being discussed inside parliaments and printed in national strategies. It's not just an investment anymore. It's an ideology. A lifeline. A quiet uprising encoded in blocks and chains.

From rebel asset to national strategy.

And behind it all are the people.

Not the politicians.
Not the bankers.

But the individuals, in every country, who decided to take control of their money and their future.

So, the question isn't:
"Will Bitcoin go mainstream?"

It already has.

The real question is:
Are you still waiting to understand it... or are you already using it?

Because this revolution doesn't knock.
It uploads.
And it's already live.

Welcome to the next era of money.

D - Doubt in centralized systems
E - Emergence of alternatives (Bitcoin, Ethereum)
F - Flow of adoption across countries & classes
I - Integration into daily life & governance

THE ROLE OF HYPERINFLATION IN CRYPTO ADOPTION

When Money Breaks, Trust Moves to the Blockchain.

"When savings lose value, people stop dreaming. But with crypto, a new hope is born."

We often think of money as something solid and stable. We earn it. We save it. We plan our future around it.

But what if, one day, your money stopped working?

What if the ₹10,000 you saved last month could buy you only ₹4,000 worth of groceries today?

What if next week, it couldn't even pay your electricity bill?

Sounds impossible?

Well, that is exactly what millions of people around the world have already experienced—from Venezuela to Zimbabwe, from Argentina to Lebanon. These countries have faced something called hyperinflation—a situation where the value of their national currency drops so fast that prices change daily, sometimes even hourly.

People in these places didn't turn to Bitcoin and crypto for investment or trading. They didn't jump in for profits.
They did it because they had no choice. Crypto became their lifeline, their last chance to protect their savings, feed their families, and stay afloat.

And now, in 2025, as inflation rises in many parts of the world—including India—people are beginning to ask:

"What if it happens to us too? What will we do when our money stops working?"

VENEZUELA: A REAL-LIFE CASE STUDY

Once one of the richest countries in South America, Venezuela is now famous for the wrong reasons. Over the past few years, their national currency—the Venezuelan bolívar—lost more than 99.9% of its value.

Imagine,
You have ₹1,00,000 in savings. And then, within a year or two, that money is worth only ₹100.
People in Venezuela couldn't buy basic food items. Salaries were worthless. Banks were unreliable. The government kept printing money, and the situation only got worse.

But the people?

They adapted.

BITCOIN AS A LIFELINE

Many Venezuelans began to use Bitcoin and stablecoins like USDT instead of their local currency.

Why?

Bitcoin doesn't lose value like their national money.
Crypto can be stored digitally, without needing a bank.
Crypto can be sent across borders instantly, which helped millions receive remittances from family members living abroad.

BUSINESSES ACCEPTING CRYPTO

From local grocery stores to large e-commerce platforms, many Venezuelan businesses began accepting Bitcoin and USDT. They preferred crypto over bolívars, simply because it held its value.
In a country where cash was losing value every hour, Bitcoin was more trustworthy.

MINING FOR SURVIVAL

Venezuela has access to cheap electricity. So many locals started mining Bitcoin using small devices. Mining became a way to earn stable income in dollars, even when local jobs didn't pay enough.

Mining helped many families survive the economic collapse. Even though the government tried to crack down on mining and crypto usage, people kept using it quietly. When trust in the government fades, people turn to math and code.

INSTITUTIONS INVOLVEMENT: FROM LAUGHING TO BUYING

For many years, large companies and financial institutions laughed at Bitcoin.

"Digital gambling," they called it.

"A passing fad."

But things changed—fast.

From 2021 to 2024, we witnessed a massive shift. The same institutions that once ignored crypto started buying billions of dollars worth of it.

Tesla

In 2021, Elon Musk's company bought $1.5 billion worth of Bitcoin and even accepted it as payment (briefly).

MicroStrategy

A U.S.-based tech company that now holds over 190,000 BTC as part of its long-term treasury. Its CEO, Michael Saylor, calls Bitcoin "digital property" and believes it's better than holding cash.

BlackRock, JP Morgan, Fidelity

These global financial giants now offer Bitcoin ETFs and crypto products to their wealthy clients. That means even the traditional finance world now respects Bitcoin as a real asset.

So, what changed?

They realized

- ❖ Inflation is not temporary.
- ❖ Fiat money is weakening.
- ❖ Bitcoin is digital gold—scarce, portable, and impossible to print.

This institutional entry gave crypto legitimacy. It also helped common people trust crypto more. If the biggest investors in the world believe in Bitcoin—maybe it's not such a crazy idea after all?

Crypto is no longer just about rich investors or software engineers. Today, it's reaching the streets, villages, and smartphones of ordinary people.

Especially in countries like India, Philippines, Vietnam, and Kenya—crypto is becoming a tool for freedom and opportunity.

THE RISE OF STABLECOINS

Bitcoin is powerful, but it's also volatile. One day it's ₹50 lakh, the next day ₹45 lakh. That's scary for someone who wants stability. That's where stablecoins come in.

USDT and USDC are cryptocurrencies pegged to the U.S. dollar. That means 1 USDT = 1 USD, almost all the time.

In countries with unstable currencies, stablecoins are becoming the new digital dollars.

In India too, freelancers and export businesses are now asking clients to pay them in USDT, because:

It's faster than a bank.
It's cheaper than PayPal.
It holds value better than the rupee.

For many, stablecoins are the first step into crypto—safe, simple, and familiar.

CRYPTO FOR PAYMENTS: FROM DREAMS TO REALITY

Earlier, you could invest in crypto, but using it for everyday payments was hard. That's changing.
Thanks to faster blockchains like Solana, Polygon, and Bitcoin's Lightning Network, you can now send and receive payments in seconds, with very low fees.

Businesses across the world—including platforms like Shopify, Starbucks, and airlines—are experimenting with crypto payments. In India, some cafes, jewellery stores, and online sellers are starting to accept Bitcoin and USDT. This trend is growing in places like Bangalore, Pune, Hyderabad, and even smaller towns.
As crypto becomes easier to use, more people will start spending it—just like they use UPI today.

PLAY-TO-EARN: GAMING BECOMES A JOB

Imagine earning ₹500–₹5,000 a week just by playing games on your phone.

That's the idea behind Play-to-Earn (P2E) games like Axie Infinity, The Sandbox, and others.

In many developing countries, young people are playing crypto games to earn income.
They can play battles or farming games.
Win crypto tokens.

Convert those tokens into cash or stablecoins.

For students, gig workers, and unemployed youth, P2E is becoming a side income stream—sometimes even a full-time job.

As Indian developers build their own Web3 games, this space could explode across our country too.

CHALLENGES ON THE ROAD TO MASS ADOPTION

Of course, every revolution faces obstacles. Crypto is powerful—but not perfect. There are some challenges that still need to be addressed.

REGULATION & LEGAL UNCERTAINTY

In India and many other countries, governments are still unsure how to regulate crypto. Some are supportive, some are cautious, and others are fearful.

The problem?
Too much regulation can kill innovation.
Too little can lead to scams and chaos.

What's needed is smart regulation—clear rules, strong consumer protection, and space for innovation. India is already working on its Crypto Bill, but there's more work to do.

Clarity will bring confidence—and help millions more Indians adopt crypto safely.

SECURITY & SCAMS

Crypto wallets give you full control of your money. But with great power comes great responsibility.

If you lose your password (private key), your crypto is gone forever.

If you fall for a scam or phishing attack, there's no customer care to help you.
That's why education is so important.

New users must learn:

- How to use wallets safely.
- How to avoid scams.
- How to store passwords securely.

Crypto is like the internet in the early days—it's powerful, but it needs digital hygiene.

SPEED & SCALABILITY

Bitcoin is secure—but slow. Ethereum is flexible—but can get expensive.

This is why new blockchain technologies are being developed that are:

- Faster (processing thousands of transactions per second)
- Cheaper (less than ₹1 per transaction)
- Scalable (able to serve millions of users without crashing)

These upgrades will make crypto more usable for the masses, not just techies.

INDIA'S WINDOW OF OPPORTUNITY

India isn't just participating in the digital age—it's leading it in its own unique way. As we stand at a historic crossroads, we hold in our hands the potential to redefine what finance means for over a billion people.

We are one of the youngest nations in the world, with an average age of just under 30. This means we're not stuck in the systems of the past—we're open to new ideas, new tools, and new possibilities. Our youth are not just digital natives; they are crypto-curious, tech-driven, and globally connected.

Add to that a staggering 850 million smartphone users, and suddenly, the entire country becomes one giant decentralized network, waiting to plug into the future. From remote villages to bustling cities, the infrastructure for a digital financial revolution is already in place—we're holding the device in our hands.

Our booming tech industry is another pillar. India isn't just using global platforms; we're building them. From software engineering to blockchain development, our homegrown talent is shaping the future of the internet itself.

But perhaps most importantly, there's something deeply Indian about the decentralized philosophy. We are a culture of savings, of innovation, of jugaad—that special knack for finding creative, low-cost solutions. When you mix that with Web3, something powerful happens.

If crypto adoption is nurtured with the right education, policy, and community support, it can unlock a flood of opportunity:

- ✓ A small business owner in Surat or Shillong could receive global payments without a middleman, using stablecoins or DeFi protocols.

- ✓ A college student in Kanpur could earn online by providing services in the metaverse or joining a DAO—no gatekeepers, no resume needed.

- ✓ A woman in rural Rajasthan could secretly and securely save money using a self-custodied wallet, giving her financial independence never offered before.

- ✓ A farmer in Bihar could access microloans through decentralized lending platforms without pleading to local moneylenders.

- ✓ Everyone, regardless of location or status, could shield themselves from future inflation by holding assets that no central bank can print at will.

Just like UPI changed India's daily life, crypto can change how we think about money itself.

The question isn't "Should India adopt crypto?"
It's:
"How fast can we do it—before another inflation wave hits?"

Because in the end, crypto is not just about profit.
It's about protection, possibility, and power—in the hands of the people.

When old money breaks, the future is built in code. And it's already here.

THE FUTURE: A BORDERLESS FINANCIAL SYSTEM?

"Imagine a world where money moves as freely as information. That world is closer than you think."

As cryptocurrency adoption accelerates, one thing becomes increasingly clear — the world is shifting toward a financial system that's decentralized, borderless, and people-powered. For the first time in history, individuals — not governments, not banks — are gaining real control over their money. And this shift isn't just happening in Silicon Valley or Wall Street. It's happening in cities like Bengaluru, villages in Bihar, and among digital nomads in Goa. It's happening in India — silently, but powerfully.

So, what does the future hold?

Will Bitcoin become the world's reserve currency, replacing the dollar as the backbone of international trade? Will governments push back with their own centralized digital currencies — the so-called CBDCs, controlled, monitored, and perhaps even weaponized against privacy? Will crypto wallets one day replace bank accounts entirely?

We don't know all the answers yet. But one thing is certain: this revolution is unstoppable.

And the only real question that remains is this:

Will you be part of it — or just a spectator watching from the sidelines?

IMAGINE: A DAY IN THE LIFE OF A CRYPTO ADOPTER IN INDIA

Let's zoom in from the macro to the micro. Let's step into the shoes of someone who's already living this decentralized dream. Meet Raj.

6:30 AM - FREEDOM IN A NOTIFICATION

The sun had just begun to rise in Bengaluru. Raj's phone buzzed with a familiar ping — a push notification from his crypto wallet.

"You've received 0.0012 BTC from @zenclient_SG."

Raj rubbed his eyes and smiled. The payment had arrived — not via a sluggish international bank wire, not through PayPal with its ridiculous fees, not via any traditional channel.

It came through Bitcoin.

No delays. No middlemen. No gatekeepers asking "why" or "from whom" or "is this compliant?"

FREEDOM FROM FINANCIAL FRICTION

Raj is a 29-year-old freelance web developer working with clients across the globe. A few years ago, he struggled constantly with payments. Getting paid from abroad was a headache. Some platforms like PayPal held funds for 21 days, citing "security checks." Banks imposed SWIFT fees, conversion fees, and GST — eating away 7–12% of every payment.

But when Raj discovered crypto, everything changed.

His Singaporean client now paid him in Bitcoin. A U.S. startup paid him in USDC. Sometimes, he even received Polygon (MATIC), developed by fellow Indians — fast, cheap, and built on Ethereum. The payments now arrived in minutes, not days. And the cost? Almost zero.

Crypto wasn't just a faster payment method for Raj. It was a new mindset — an escape from outdated, colonial-era financial systems that were never built for people like him.

9:00 AM – SPENDING CRYPTO IN THE REAL WORLD

Later that morning, Raj opened an app that allowed him to spend crypto directly — not just online, but at physical stores too. Some grocery stores in his neighborhood now accepted payments in stablecoins through QR codes. Even where they didn't, he could use crypto-linked prepaid cards that converted instantly.

Buying a cup of chai or filling up his fuel tank didn't require him to liquidate crypto on an exchange anymore. It was seamless. Normal.

And it was just the beginning.

1:00 PM – INVESTING WITHOUT MIDDLEMEN

During his lunch break, Raj checked a DeFi (Decentralized Finance) platform. He'd put a portion of his savings into a lending pool where he earned interest daily — all without needing a bank, broker, or government approval. No paperwork. No KYC delays. Just his crypto wallet, a few clicks, and full transparency.

"Why wait for banks to approve a fixed deposit," he thought, "when I can earn 8% APY on a stablecoin right now?"

To Raj, DeFi was more than passive income. It was an education. It taught him how financial systems worked — and how broken they often were.

3:00 PM – PRIVACY AND OWNERSHIP

Raj received a call from a journalist friend working on a story about CBDCs — Central Bank Digital Currencies. As the Indian government pilots the Digital Rupee, many are celebrating it as a sign of progress. But Raj had concerns.

"CBDCs might be programmable money," he explained, "but what if it's also surveillance money?"

He wasn't paranoid. Just realistic.

What if the government limited how much you could spend in a month? What if they froze funds based on your social media posts? With crypto, Raj felt ownership. With CBDCs, he feared control.

Crypto, after all, isn't just money. It's a philosophy — one that says you deserve privacy, autonomy, and choice.

7:00 PM – COMMUNITY AND CREATION

As the day wound down, Raj joined a Twitter Space where fellow Indians were discussing the latest NFT trends. One creator from Mumbai had just sold a digital painting for $12,000 to a collector in Brazil. Another speaker shared how DAOs (Decentralized Autonomous Organizations) were funding clean water projects in rural India.

Crypto wasn't just about investment. It was about connection — to ideas, people, causes, and missions across the globe. Raj wasn't just consuming content; he was creating, sharing, and building.

10:00 PM – LOOKING AHEAD

Before sleeping, Raj opened his crypto portfolio again. Bitcoin was down 2% since morning.

But he didn't panic.

He remembered what he'd learned — crypto wasn't a get-rich-quick scheme. It was a slow, powerful shift from centralized systems to open networks. It was messy. Volatile. Experimental. But it was honest.

And it was his.

Raj's day might sound futuristic. But it's already real for thousands of Indians — coders, artists, students, migrants, freelancers, farmers. People from all walks of life are slowly stepping out of traditional systems that excluded them and into new ones that empower them.

Yes, challenges remain. Scams, regulatory confusion, and misinformation still plague the industry. But what we're witnessing isn't a trend. It's a transformation.

This isn't just about coins and tokens.

It's about redefining what it means to trust, to trade, to transact.

It's about tearing down gates and building bridges.

India is at a crossroads. With the youngest population in the world, unmatched digital connectivity, and a legacy of innovation — we have the chance to not just adopt crypto, but to lead it.

But revolutions aren't won by governments. They're driven by people. People like Raj. People like you.

You don't need a finance degree.
You don't need to be a coder.
You don't even need a lot of money.

All you need is curiosity — and the courage to imagine a better financial future.

Because in this new world, you don't need anyone's permission to participate.

You just need a wallet — and a vision.

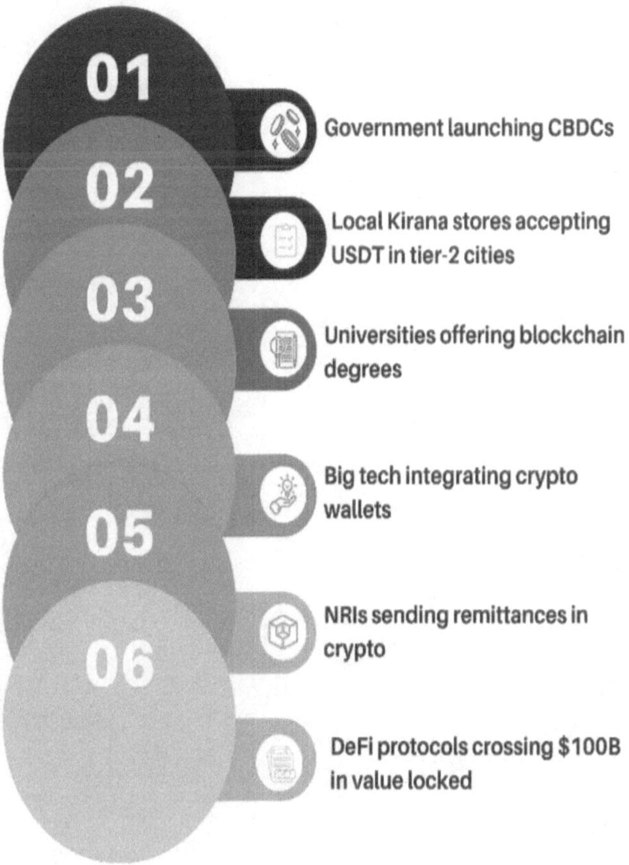

SIGNALS THAT ADOPTION IS REAL

REALITY: THE DREAM OF BORDERLESS FINANCE

Think about this: In 2025, you can send an email from Delhi to Tokyo in a split second. You can video call someone in London from your village in Kerala without paying a rupee. You can stream music made by an artist in Argentina while sipping chai in Kolkata.

But when it comes to money?

Try sending ₹5,000 to a friend in the US. You'll go through:

- High conversion rates
- Bank paperwork
- 2–4-day delays
- And hefty fees

In a world where information is instant, why is money still stuck behind borders, banks, and bureaucracy?

The answer lies in how financial systems have evolved. And the solution? It might just be crypto, blockchain, and decentralized finance (DeFi)—together paving the way for a truly borderless financial system.

The most powerful revolutions don't come with noise—they come with integration. When people stop asking, 'What is Bitcoin?' and start using it without thinking, that's true adoption."

WHAT IS A BORDERLESS FINANCIAL SYSTEM?

At its core, a borderless financial system is a world where:

- You can send money anywhere, instantly.
- You don't need permission from a bank or government.

- Your money isn't limited by currency, geography, or political rules.

It's a system that works 24/7, with no central authority, and minimal fees.

Think of it like the internet of money—free, fast, global, and inclusive.

Now, compare that to our current system:

- Cross-border transactions take 3–7 days.
- Bank charges are high (especially for the poor).
- Millions of people don't even have a bank account.
- International finance is controlled by a handful of powerful institutions.

This isn't just unfair—it's outdated.

A borderless system promises to change that forever.

WHY THE CURRENT FINANCIAL SYSTEM IS BROKEN

Imagine Raj—a 25-year-old software developer living in the tech capital of India, Bengaluru. Like many in his generation, Raj is smart, digital-first, and deeply connected to his family back home in Tamil Nadu. His cousin, Arjun, works in Dubai and sends money home every month to support their parents and cover expenses.

It sounds simple. But every time Arjun hits 'Send,' a slow and expensive maze begins.

He sends ₹1,000—but only about ₹930 actually reaches Raj's bank account after conversion fees and service charges. That's ₹70 lost for nothing but gatekeepers. The transaction takes 2–3 business days—sometimes more if there's a weekend, a bank holiday, or a random system error. And let's not forget the paperwork, the government scrutiny, and the nagging feeling that someone is always watching.

It's not illegal money. But somehow, it feels like privacy has become a luxury.

Now picture this same transaction through crypto. Arjun opens his crypto wallet in Dubai, sends ₹1,000 worth of USDT or Bitcoin. In less than five minutes, Raj gets a ping — "Funds received." No banks. No red tape. No delays. And not a single rupee lost to conversion or commission.

It doesn't matter whether it's midnight, a Sunday, or a national holiday. The money is there. Safe. Direct. Borderless.

This isn't science fiction. It's the difference between a system still operating like a typewriter—and a solution built for the smartphone era.

Crypto doesn't just offer speed or convenience.
It offers control.
It offers fairness.
It offers freedom in a world where even money has started feeling... monitored.

For people like Raj and Arjun, the broken system isn't just a theory. It's their reality. And crypto? It's no longer an option. It's the upgrade they've been waiting for.

WHAT MAKES BLOCKCHAIN THE RIGHT TECHNOLOGY?

Blockchain is the backbone of the borderless financial revolution.

Here's why it works so well:

- **Decentralization** – No central bank or institution controls it. Power is shared.

- **Transparency** – Every transaction is recorded publicly. No hidden charges.

- **Security** – Once data is added, it can't be changed. Fraud becomes very hard.

- **Accessibility** – All you need is a phone and internet to join the system.

For the first time in human history, people can exchange value globally without asking for permission.

It's like when the printing press gave books to everyone. Or when the internet gave information to everyone. Blockchain is giving finance to everyone.

HOW IS IT ALREADY WORKING AROUND THE WORLD?

This isn't science fiction. Borderless finance is already real.

Let's look at examples:

PHILIPPINES

Over 11 million Filipinos work overseas. They send billions home. But the fees are high. That's why many families are switching to USDT and Bitcoin remittances. It's faster, cheaper, and reliable.

ARGENTINA

With 100% inflation, locals have lost trust in their peso. Many now store wealth in Bitcoin or stablecoins. Teens earn crypto through online work and avoid local banks altogether.

NIGERIA

Young Nigerians are building entire businesses using crypto wallets. From art to fashion to freelance services, they get paid in crypto, bypassing unstable local systems.

INDIA (the rising star)

- ❖ Freelancers now prefer USDT to avoid PayPal delays.
- ❖ Students in tier-2 cities are investing through DeFi apps.
- ❖ NRIs are sending remittances in crypto to family back home.

It's happening. Quietly. Rapidly. Irreversibly.

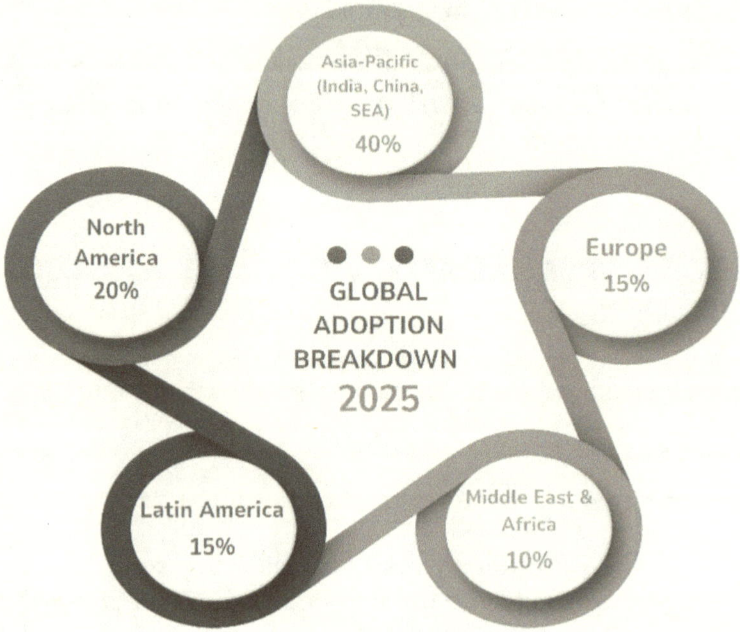

THE RISE OF STABLECOINS: THE DIGITAL DOLLAR FOR ALL

Bitcoin is powerful, but it fluctuates in price.

Enter stablecoins—cryptocurrencies like USDT (Tether) and USDC (Circle) that are pegged to the value of the U.S. dollar.

Stablecoins are the fuel of borderless finance. Why?

- ❖ They don't swing wildly in price.

- You can use them like cash—send, receive, save.
- They work 24/7. No banks required.

For someone in a small town in Odisha, a stablecoin is like holding dollars in their phone. No forex fees. No paperwork. Just value they can use globally.

THE ROLE OF DEFI (DECENTRALIZED FINANCE)

DeFi is like rebuilding the whole financial system—from banks to insurance to loans—on the blockchain.

Here's what DeFi lets you do:

- Get a loan without going to a bank.
- Earn interest on your crypto (more than FD rates!).
- Trade, invest, and borrow—all from your phone.

In a borderless system, DeFi apps replace traditional banks.

Imagine Ravi, a small business owner in Rajasthan, needs a loan. The local bank says no. But Ravi can use DeFi to borrow against crypto—no credit score needed, no forms.

That's freedom. That's borderless. That's the future.

DIGITAL IDENTITY AND FINANCIAL INCLUSION

Let's take a journey to a small village in Jharkhand. Life moves at its own rhythm here—quiet, beautiful, but far from the digital highways of urban India. In this village lives Anika, a young woman who runs a small tailoring business from her home. She's hardworking, sharp, and ambitious. But there's one problem: she has no bank account.
And she's not alone.

Across the globe, over 1.7 billion people remain unbanked—cut off from the formal financial system.
Why?
The reasons are painfully simple.
They don't have a government-issued ID.
They live in remote or rural regions.
And for traditional banks, they're just not "profitable enough" to serve.

Now here's where the story begins to change.

Because crypto doesn't ask for permission.

There are no bank forms to fill, no waiting in line, no need for Aadhaar or voter ID. If you have a smartphone, you can have a crypto wallet—instantly. Just like that, Anika can send and receive payments, save money securely, and even access online earning opportunities from her own home.

But it doesn't stop there.

The future holds something even more powerful: blockchain-based digital identity systems.
With them, Anika can one day prove who she is online, own her credentials, and access microloans or insurance policies from lenders across the globe—without ever stepping into a bank.

From tribal communities in Madhya Pradesh to the highlands of Himachal, a quiet financial revolution is taking shape. A revolution where your location doesn't limit your potential. Where identity is portable, private, and powered by code.

This is the promise of decentralization: a financial system that includes—not excludes.
And for people like Anika, it's not just inclusion.
It's empowerment.

CROSS-BORDER TRADE WITHOUT BORDERS

Businesses spend billions on:

- Currency conversion
- SWIFT transfers
- International bank delays

With crypto and blockchain, they can:

- Pay suppliers instantly
- Receive international payments in stablecoins
- Automate customs using smart contracts

Imagine a saree seller in Varanasi shipping to Germany and receiving instant payment in USDC. That's global e-commerce without banks.

GOVERNMENTS AND CBDCS: WILL THEY JOIN OR FIGHT?

Some governments fear crypto. But many are now launching CBDCs (Central Bank Digital Currencies)—digital versions of their currency.

India's Digital Rupee is one example.

CBDCs are not borderless, but they're a step forward.

The real question is: Will governments allow people to use Bitcoin, stablecoins, and DeFi, or will they force only their own digital currency?

The answer will shape the next decade of finance.

But the truth is: the internet never asked for permission to exist. Crypto won't either.

CHALLENGES AHEAD

Let's be honest. There are real obstacles:

- ✓ **Scams & Hacks** – Education is needed to keep users safe.
- ✓ **Volatility** – Coins like Bitcoin swing in price, making them hard to use daily.
- ✓ **Energy Use** – Some blockchain systems use a lot of electricity (though newer ones are greener).
- ✓ **Regulatory Confusion** – Governments need to balance innovation and control.

But remember: The internet also had problems. It didn't stop progress. It evolved. So will crypto.

CRYPTO ADOPTION VELOCITY (CAV)

CAV = (Digital Access × Economic Need) / (Regulatory Resistance + Tech Literacy Gap)

Where:

- ❖ **Digital Access** = smartphone + internet penetration
- ❖ **Economic Need** = inflation, remittance dependency
- ❖ **Regulatory Resistance** = strict laws, unclear policy
- ❖ **Tech Literacy Gap** = awareness and access issues

This equation helps explain why countries with high economic need and digital access but low regulatory resistance adopts crypto faster.

A World Without Borders Isn't a Dream. It's a Destination.

Money doesn't have to be slow.
It doesn't have to be expensive.
It doesn't have to be unfair.

With blockchain, DeFi, and crypto,

You own your money

You control your financial life

You connect with the world freely

The borderless financial system isn't coming.

It's already here.

And it's waiting for you to log in.

*****

"The Metaverse is not about being inside the internet, it's about the internet being inside of us—an economy without borders."

©Mark Zuckerberg

CHAPTER FIVE

THE METAVERSE ECONOMY – A NEW DIGITAL WORLD WITHOUT BORDERS

"The metaverse isn't a place. It's a shift in power – from physical borders to digital ownership."
– Inspired by Vitalik Buterin

Hyderabad, 2035,

A Day in the Life of Sanya in the Metaverse Economy.

It was a regular morning in Hyderabad. The city was waking up, the birds were singing outside, and the early sun was shining gently through the window of Sanya's apartment in a quiet, modern neighborhood. She sat on her couch, holding her cup of chai. But unlike most people, she wasn't in a rush to catch a bus or rush through traffic. Instead, she reached for her sleek VR headset.

With one smooth motion, she placed it over her eyes, and just like that—she was no longer in her living room. She had entered the Metaverse.

No traffic. No long drives. No office buildings. Just a beautiful, digital world where her job, her office, and her entire career now lived.

Her workspace was not a boring cubicle with grey walls. It was a virtual dome, surrounded by glowing trees and rivers made of data. The walls changed color based on her mood, and the soft sound of wind played in the background. This was not just cool—it was peaceful, creative, and powerful.

Her colleagues arrived a few moments later. There was Hiro, a software developer from Japan. Lena, a marketing expert from Germany. And Miguel, a data analyst from the U.S. All of them appeared as avatars—digital versions of themselves. They smiled, waved, and began their workday just like she did.

Their office? A beautiful 3D environment full of floating screens, smart AI assistants, and real-time data all around them. They could design, brainstorm, and run campaigns—all from their homes in different countries.

Their salaries? All paid in *Ethereum*.

A JOB WITHOUT BORDERS

Sanya's job was simple: help brands grow in the Metaverse. One of their current clients, a natural skincare company, wanted to launch a global campaign using Web3 tools like NFTs, smart contracts, and immersive 3D events.

Sanya reviewed the campaign plan, made some updates to the code, and used hand gestures to adjust visuals floating in front of her. It was like being a magician, moving shapes and data in the air.

She loved how fast everything worked. There were no boring emails or approvals. She clicked a button, and the smart contract handled the rest. Everyone in the team could see the changes in real time. The client was happy, and just like that—payment was released automatically to her wallet.

No waiting for salary day. No bank problems.

She smiled. This wasn't just work. It was freedom.

Two decades ago, her parents had a different life. Her father used to leave the house at 8 AM, travel for over an hour through traffic, sit at a desk for nine hours, and come home tired. Her mother worked at a government bank, where even small tasks took days because of paper files and approvals.

Sanya's life was the opposite. She worked from home, chose her own hours, and earned more than what her parents ever imagined. All she needed was a VR headset, an internet connection, and her skills.

And her boss? She didn't really have one.

Her work spoke for itself.

BREAKS IN THE METAVERSE

Around lunch, Sanya took a break. But instead of watching TV or scrolling through social media, she joined a virtual art gallery inside Decentraland. There, digital paintings by artists from Africa, Brazil, and Kerala were on display.

She liked one abstract piece showing a dancing robot and decided to buy it as an NFT. In less than a minute, she paid using Ethereum and added the art to her virtual collection. She could even hang it in her virtual home—or rent it out during events.

Later, she visited a music show where a Brazilian DJ was performing live. Thousands of people from all over the world were watching and dancing with their avatars. It was like a global party—without even stepping outside.

TEACHING IN THE EVENING

In the evening, Sanya decided to give back. She opened a virtual classroom and invited a few students from India. They wanted to learn how to create digital clothes for avatars. Sanya, once a fashion student herself, showed them how to design, mint, and sell wearable NFTs.

Her students asked, "Can we earn from this?"

She smiled and said, "You don't need to go abroad to succeed anymore. The world is already here, on your screen."

She felt proud. Not just for what she had achieved—but for what others could now dream of.

LOGGING OFF, FEELING FREE

As night fell, Sanya took off her headset and sat quietly on her balcony. Hyderabad was still the same outside. The traffic lights, the chai stalls, the sounds of scooters buzzing by.

But she was living in a different world—a digital one.

She opened her phone and checked her wallet. Her crypto savings had grown. She had enough to pay her bills, invest in a few NFTs, and even save for a trip to Goa next month—both in real life and in the metaverse. This wasn't some future dream. This was her normal.

She thought of the millions of young people across India who were still stuck in old systems—waiting for results, chasing jobs, or standing in long queues.

And then she thought of those who had started exploring the Metaverse—building careers as creators, gamers, designers, and community leaders. Just like her.

It's not science fiction. It's not a game. It's real. And it's here.

In this new economy:

- You don't need to live in a big city to find a good job.
- You don't need to ask permission to earn.
- You don't need to follow old rules to create new things.

If you have a skill, an internet connection, and a little curiosity—you can be part of it.

Like Sanya.

A girl from Hyderabad, living in a simple flat, building a global career—all from her room.

This is the Metaverse Economy.

And the best part?

It belongs to you.

WHAT IS THE METAVERSE, REALLY?

When you hear the word "Metaverse," what comes to your mind? Maybe futuristic cities with flying cars. Maybe a video game. Or maybe just a confusing buzzword used by tech people.

But what if I told you that the Metaverse isn't just a fantasy or a trend? It's not science fiction anymore. It's the next version of the internet. And slowly, it's becoming part of real life.

To understand the Metaverse economy, the jobs it brings, and the opportunities it creates, we first need to understand what this "Metaverse" really is.

So, let's take a step back and start from the beginning.
Not Just Another Internet—A New Digital Universe.

Think about how we use the internet today. We open a browser, search for something, maybe read an article, watch a video, or shop online. We scroll. We click. We type. It's all happening on a screen, in 2D.

Now imagine if, instead of looking at a screen, you stepped into the internet. Literally.

You wear your VR headset, and suddenly, you're no longer sitting in your bedroom—you're inside a digital world. You're walking down a virtual street; your avatar dressed just the way you like. You visit a digital store, try on some shoes, buy them using digital currency, and chat with a friend—all inside that world.

This is the Metaverse. Not a single website. Not a single app. But a network of digital spaces where people can live, work, play, learn, and earn.
Just like the internet has many websites, the Metaverse has many worlds.

Some are fully immersive 3D platforms like Decentraland or The Sandbox, where you can buy digital land, build homes, and host events. Others are more like games—Roblox, Minecraft, or Fortnite—where people come together to play and create. And then there are professional spaces like Horizon Workrooms or Microsoft Mesh, where companies hold meetings and work together inside digital rooms.

Each one is different. But all of them are part of this larger digital universe—the Metaverse.

You Don't Just Watch. You Live Inside. The biggest change the Metaverse brings is this: it's not about just watching things. It's about being part of them.

Let's say you're attending a music concert. On YouTube, you watch it on a screen. But in the Metaverse? You walk into a huge virtual stadium. You dance with other fans, wave at the performer, and maybe even buy a digital T-shirt—an NFT—that proves you were there.

Or think about shopping. In today's world, you click on clothes, scroll through pictures, and hope they fit. In the Metaverse, your avatar walks into a virtual boutique, tries on outfits, and sees how they look from every angle.

Even work is changing. You don't send emails or video calls anymore. You sit in a digital meeting room, side by side with your teammates—represented by avatars. You brainstorm, share files, and work together—almost like you're in the same real-world office.

In the Metaverse, you're not browsing. You're existing inside the experience.

And this changes everything.

REAL OWNERSHIP—EVEN IF IT'S DIGITAL

One of the most powerful ideas behind the Metaverse is digital ownership.

Let's say you buy a painting in the real world. You can hang it in your house. It belongs to you. But on the internet, ownership is tricky. You can download a photo, but so can everyone else.

Now, thanks to blockchain technology, digital ownership is possible.

Through NFTs (non-fungible tokens), you can own a piece of art, a song, a plot of land, or even a shirt your avatar wears. These items are recorded on the blockchain—so everyone knows you own them, and nobody can fake it.

This creates a whole new economy. People are:

- Buying and selling digital land.
- Creating and trading avatar clothing.

- ❖ Performing concerts and charging ticket prices in crypto.
- ❖ Opening virtual schools, offices, shops, even nightclubs.

And here's the amazing part—it's not just big companies doing this.

It's individuals. Creators. Freelancers. Teenagers in small towns. Artists in villages. Teachers in cities. All of them are finding real value in digital spaces.

REAL PEOPLE, REAL INCOME

A few years ago, it would've sounded strange to say, "I make a living by designing clothes for digital characters" or "I built a café inside a video game, and I rent it out to global brands."

But today? It's happening.

In India, the Metaverse is opening doors for young people like never before.

A student in Delhi sells custom fashion NFTs for avatars. A graphic designer in Jaipur creates art galleries inside Decentraland. A coder in Hyderabad works on smart contracts for Metaverse land sales. A musician in Chennai performs weekly shows in a digital club—and people attend from all around the world.

What's even more interesting is that these people often earn in cryptocurrency—Bitcoin, Ethereum, or stablecoins like USDT. It doesn't matter where they live. Their clients can be in Japan, Germany, or Brazil. The payments are fast, borderless, and completely digital.

This is not just the internet of content.

This is the internet of opportunity.

VIRTUAL REAL ESTATE: THE NEXT FRONTIER

One of the strangest (yet exciting) ideas in the Metaverse is this: you can own land.

Yes, digital land.

Inside platforms like The Sandbox or Decentraland, people can buy virtual plots. These are limited in number—just like real land. And they're not just empty spaces. People build homes, offices, stores, art galleries, even schools on them.

In 2021, one virtual land plot sold for over 2 million USD.

That's the power of belief—and the potential of the Metaverse. People believe these spaces are valuable because they're social, creative, and full of life. And every day, more and more users are coming in.

A SOCIETY WITHOUT BORDERS

In the Metaverse, your passport doesn't matter. Your location doesn't matter. What matters is what you bring to the table—your skills, your creativity, your energy.

Here, you can:

- Work for a company in Canada from a village in Kerala.
- Teach a class to kids in Australia from a flat in Bhopal.
- Sell digital sneakers to gamers in New York from your hostel room in Lucknow.

Borders disappear. Platforms become countries. Communities become nations.

And the rules are changing, too.

You don't need to wear a suit to work. Your avatar can wear a neon jacket with dragon wings if that's your vibe. You don't need to wait years for promotions. You can start your own business on day one. You don't need anyone's permission to create.

It's a world of freedom. A world of self-expression. A world where the economy belongs to the people—not just the platforms.

The Metaverse Is Not Coming. It's Already Here.

Some might still call the Metaverse a dream. But for thousands of people across the world—including many in India—it's already part of daily life.

It's where they earn. It's where they socialize. It's where they build their future.

And the best part?

You can still be early.

This is the beginning of something huge. Something global.

Something that could change how we live, work, and play forever.

So, whether you're a student, a creator, a gamer, a teacher, or just someone curious—this digital universe is waiting.

The only question is: *will you step in?*

HOW INDIA IS LEADING THE METAVERSE REVOLUTION

In a quiet village in Tamil Nadu, an old farmer logs into a virtual market using his smartphone. His grandson helps him navigate the app. A few taps later, they've listed their fresh organic produce on a global platform, visible to buyers from Dubai to Denmark. Payment? It arrives in USDT within minutes.

Meanwhile, across the country in Mumbai, a young film director is sipping chai in his living room, while thousands of fans from around the world line up—inside a virtual theatre—to watch his latest short film premiere in the Metaverse. The audience isn't just watching—they're buying NFT movie posters, joining live Q&A sessions, and collecting digital souvenirs of their favourite scenes.

This is not fiction.

This is India's Metaverse moment.

FROM IT HUBS TO VIRTUAL WORLDS: A NATION TRANSFORMS

India has always been at the forefront of digital evolution. From becoming the IT outsourcing capital of the world to launching UPI, one of the most advanced digital payment systems, the country has shown time and again that it can leapfrog into the future.

But now, something even bigger is happening.

India isn't just following the Metaverse wave.

It's helping shape it.

With over 700 million internet users, a young and ambitious population, and an ever-growing army of Web3 developers, creators, and entrepreneurs, India is becoming one of the most exciting players in the global Metaverse economy.

And it's happening everywhere—from big cities to small villages, from tech parks to farmland.

MUMBAI: WHERE BOLLYWOOD MEETS BLOCKCHAIN

It's impossible to talk about culture in India without mentioning Bollywood. Mumbai, the heart of India's film industry, is now taking bold steps into the Metaverse.

Imagine this: instead of going to a cinema to watch a movie, fans around the world enter a digital stadium where they meet their favourite actors—virtually. Posters, behind-the-scenes footage, music tracks, and movie clips are all released as NFTs. These aren't just collectibles. They are assets—rare, ownable, and tradeable.

Fans are no longer just viewers. They are owners of pieces of their favourite films. And artists? They're no longer trapped in contracts with production houses. They earn directly from their audience.

In 2025, a young indie filmmaker from Mumbai released her debut film exclusively in Decentraland. The film was only accessible to users who bought an NFT ticket. Within 24 hours, she earned more than she would have in two years working under traditional studio deals.

Bollywood stars, singers, producers, and writers are beginning to tokenize their work, build communities on platforms like Discord and Spatial, and host virtual meet-and-greets that generate revenue and fan engagement like never before.

BENGALURU: INDIA'S SILICON VALLEY TURNS META

Bengaluru—India's tech capital—is already known for its brilliant coders, startups, and global tech companies. But now, it's also becoming one of the key innovation zones for the Metaverse.

Here, companies are doing more than just "adopting" Metaverse tools—they're building the infrastructure for it.

Startup offices that once existed in glass buildings are now being replaced by virtual campuses. Employees log in as avatars. Meetings take place inside immersive boardrooms. Team lunches happen on a floating island in a digital world.

And it's not just fun—it's effective.

Many Indian tech firms, especially post-pandemic, have created fully remote teams that use platforms like Spatial, Gather, and Horizon Workrooms to connect employees from around the globe.

Engineers in Pune collaborate with designers in Poland. AI trainers in Chennai brainstorm with blockchain architects in Canada. Geography no longer matters. Talent rules.

One Bengaluru-based company even set up a virtual hiring fair. Hundreds of job seekers explored booths inside a 3D world, chatted with HR managers via avatars, and submitted resumes using NFT access passes.

This is work without walls—and Bengaluru is showing the world how it's done.

DELHI: STARTUPS BUILD THE FUTURE OF DIGITAL BUSINESS

Delhi, the capital of India, is known for its political power and business energy. Now, it's adding another title to its name: Metaverse Startup Central.

Here, young entrepreneurs are launching companies that exist completely in the digital world. From virtual malls to Metaverse banks, they're creating platforms where users can shop, learn, and even open accounts—all inside immersive environments.

Want to attend a music concert with your friends from three different countries? You can. Want to go to a business conference with speakers from five continents? Done. All you need is a headset—or even just a browser.

And the access system? It's run using NFTs.

Startups in Delhi are experimenting with NFT-based ticketing systems, digital storefronts that mirror real ones, and even decentralized event spaces where users can host private parties, weddings, and workshops.

One education startup launched its own Metaverse university, where students can attend live lectures in a digital auditorium, interact with classmates, and complete assignments while exploring a gamified learning world.

The lines between real and virtual? They're blurring fast—and Delhi's innovators are the ones behind it.

INDIA'S VILLAGES: A SILENT REVOLUTION UNFOLDS

Perhaps the most beautiful part of this story lies not in big cities, but in India's quiet, green villages.

Places often left out of digital revolutions are now finding new economic power through the Metaverse.

In Punjab and Tamil Nadu, farmers are exploring Metaverse marketplaces where they can list their crops for global buyers.

Smart contracts ensure they're paid fairly and quickly—without middlemen.

In Rajasthan and Kerala, artists and craftspeople are setting up virtual galleries. They upload 3D versions of their work, set prices in cryptocurrency, and reach collectors from around the world.

One group of weavers from a tribal community in Odisha uploaded a digital version of their saree patterns onto an NFT platform. Within a week, they had sales from five countries. The earnings? More than what they would've made in six months locally.

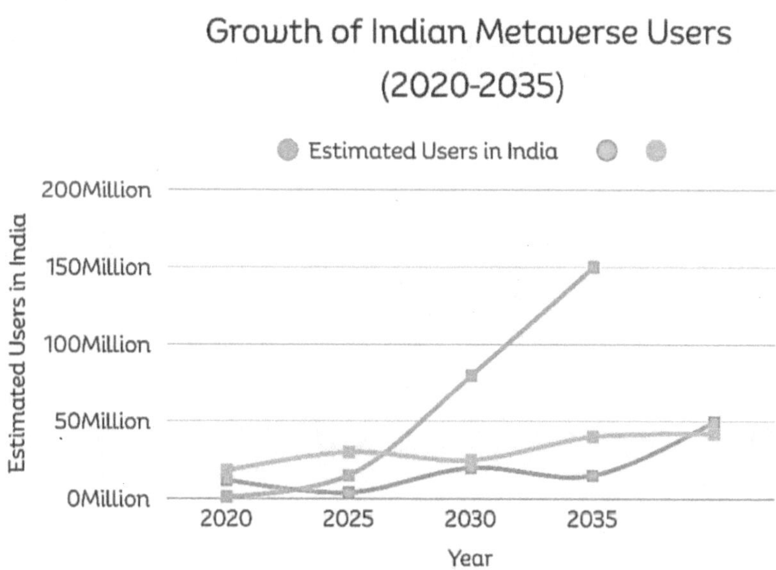

Source: Illustrative data for conceptual use

It's not just about money.

It's about dignity, reach, and independence.

The Metaverse isn't a rich man's toy. It's a bridge for every Indian with a phone and a dream.

THE METAVERSE IS BECOMING INDIA'S EQUALIZER

What makes India's role in the Metaverse so unique is diversity.

In one part of the country, a teenager is building games inside Roblox.

In another, a grandmother is using her crypto wallet to support her grandchildren's education.

A student in Lucknow earns Ethereum by creating Metaverse wearables.

A group of DJs in Manipur throw weekly VR parties attended by fans from Australia and Japan.

It's not just about business, or entertainment, or education—it's about all of it, happening at once, with Indians from every corner leading the charge.

WHAT MAKES INDIA SO READY FOR THE METAVERSE?

There are a few key reasons:

- ✓ **Demographics**: Over 65% of India's population is under 35. They're digital natives. They've grown up with smartphones, gaming, and the internet. The Metaverse feels natural to them.
- ✓ **Tech Talent**: Indian developers, artists, animators, and engineers are already powering many global Web3 projects. From coding smart contracts to designing NFTs—they're in demand.
- ✓ **Startups and Innovation**: India is home to one of the world's most active startup ecosystems. New ideas, quick pivots, and fearless founders are building India's Web3 future.

- **Government Push for Digital India**: While crypto regulations are still developing, the government has strongly supported digital transformation—from Aadhaar to UPI to ONDC.

All of this creates the perfect storm for a country ready to lead the Metaverse revolution—not in theory, but in action.

FROM PARTICIPATION TO LEADERSHIP

India isn't just showing up in the Metaverse.

It's building it.

From small-town creators to Bollywood stars, from techies to teachers, from startup founders to rural artists—everyone is carving out space in this digital world.

The Metaverse is not a trend.

It's a tool.

A tool that's giving Indians the power to create, earn, and connect beyond borders.

So, whether you're a coder, a designer, a musician, or a farmer—your passport to the Metaverse is already in your pocket.

All you need is vision.

And India? India has plenty of that.

HOW PEOPLE ARE EARNING IN THE METAVERSE ECONOMY

The metaverse isn't just a cool digital world anymore—it's becoming a real place where people are working, earning, and even building careers. From tier-2 towns to metro cities, Indians are quietly tapping into this new economy—and it's just getting started.

Believe it or not, people are buying digital land just like plots in Gurgaon or Navi Mumbai. In places like Decentraland and The Sandbox, Indians are purchasing small virtual plots and either flipping them later at a higher price or renting them out to brands who want to set up virtual shops. One guy from Jaipur bought land for just ₹20,000 and later sold it for ₹4 lakhs. All digital. All real money.

Then there's Gaming as a Career. Remember when our parents said "you can't earn by playing video games"? Well, times have changed. Now, games like Axie Infinity, Zed Run, and others actually *pay you* to play. College students in places like Indore and Kochi are playing these "play-to-earn" games and making monthly side incomes. Some are even using this to pay for tuition or help at home. No boss, no office—just a good internet connection.

And it's not just gaming. There are Real Jobs in the Metaverse too. Think about designing a virtual wedding mandap, managing a virtual concert for Holi, or giving a guided avatar tour of the Taj Mahal. People in India are already becoming virtual architects, 3D designers, event managers, and community moderators for global projects—working from home, but for international clients.

Now let's talk about Digital Art, Fashion & Virtual Goods. Indian artists are minting their art as NFTs and selling them to collectors worldwide. A designer from Mumbai created digital sarees for avatars—and they sold out within hours. Fashion is going digital, and so is creativity. Musicians, doodle artists, and illustrators are now showcasing their work inside the metaverse—and getting paid in crypto.

Even Education in the Metaverse is taking off. A Hindi teacher from Lucknow created an avatar and started teaching NRIs online through metaverse classrooms. Yoga instructors, coding coaches, and financial mentors are creating virtual learning hubs and reaching students in the US, Dubai, or even Japan—without ever leaving their home in India.

The best part? You don't need to be a tech genius. You just need a skill, a smartphone or laptop, and the curiosity to explore.

The metaverse is opening doors that didn't exist before. It doesn't care if you live in a big city or a small village. In this new digital world, your talent—not your location—matters the most.

And this is just the beginning.

DIGITAL LAND AND THE RISE OF VIRTUAL REAL ESTATE

It was a quiet evening in Jaipur. The monsoon rain tapped gently against the windows, and Kunal, a 26-year-old interior designer, sat in his room—laptop open, chai in hand. But unlike others scrolling Instagram or watching Netflix, Kunal was walking through the streets of Decentraland.

He wasn't just exploring. He was hunting for land.

Digital land.

Just five years ago, the idea of buying land in a virtual world would've sounded absurd. "Who would pay for something they can't touch?" people would ask. But today, the rules of the game had changed. And Kunal was living proof.

He had bought his first digital plot in 2027 for ₹12,000, using saved-up freelance earnings. It was a small corner space near a popular plaza in The Sandbox. At first, he wasn't sure what to do with it. But he decorated it with simple 3D furniture, created a virtual café space, and added some NFT art on the walls. Within weeks, visitors started coming in—some out of curiosity, others to hang out in the social zone.

Then one day, a startup from Singapore messaged him.

"Hey, are you willing to lease this spot for a product launch?"

That message changed everything. From a designer with inconsistent clients, Kunal had suddenly become a landlord in a world without physical limits. The lease earned him 800 USDT. That was more than what he made in a whole month from his traditional clients.

Soon, he bought more land—one in Decentraland, another in Voxels. Every plot was a new opportunity: an art gallery here, a rooftop party venue there. He collaborated with 3D artists, hosted events, even rented space for a Metaverse music night.

By 2030, his original ₹12,000 investment was worth ₹4.8 lakh.

But Kunal wasn't alone.

Across India, people were beginning to understand the magic of digital real estate. In Mumbai, ad agencies opened virtual billboards in high-traffic Metaverse zones. In Hyderabad, tech firms hosted job fairs in floating auditoriums. And in Kochi, wedding planners organized virtual ceremonies for NRI families spread across continents.

Land in the Metaverse wasn't just code. It was experience. It was imagination. It was economy.

And with NFTs as proof of ownership, people could sell, lease, and transfer property without lawyers or brokers. No stamp duty, no paperwork—just your wallet and a secure blockchain.

Back in Jaipur, Kunal was sipping his second chai. He smiled as his phone pinged again.

Another lease inquiry. Another opportunity.

He had found his place in the new world. Not by moving to Mumbai or Silicon Valley—but by buying land in a place that didn't even exist on the map.

Digital Land ROI = (Purchase Price + Design Layer + Brand Activation) → 2x–10x value in resell or rent

GAMING AS A CAREER – NOT JUST FUN ANYMORE

Let's take you 2,000 kilometers away to a small town in Assam. Here lives Riya, a 19-year-old girl who always loved games. Mobile games, PC games, console games—if it had a screen and a story, she was hooked.

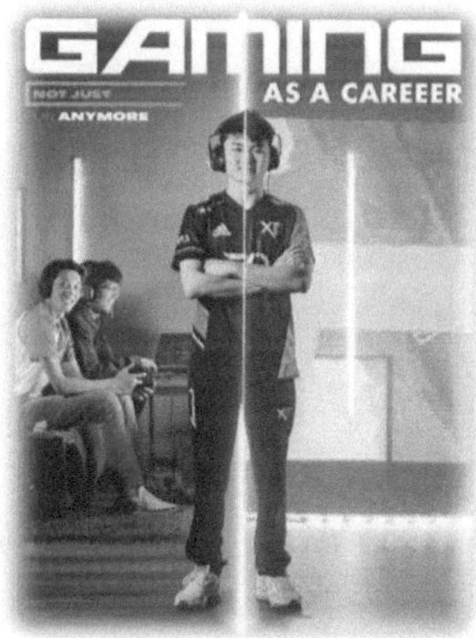

Her parents weren't fans of her "wasting time." They wanted her to become a teacher, or maybe work at a bank.

But everything changed when Riya discovered a game called Axie Infinity.

It was early 2025. She read online that this game allowed players to earn money while battling little creatures called Axies. It sounded like a scam. But something told her to try.

She borrowed ₹6,000 from her uncle to buy her first three Axies. The learning curve was steep at first—training, battling, upgrading, trading. But within a month, she had already made back her investment. By the second month, she was earning over ₹18,000. Every month.

She didn't stop there.

She joined a gaming guild—a team of players who shared tips, strategies, and earnings. She took part in tournaments, learned about NFTs, and began flipping rare Axie items for profit.

Then came the real moment of pride.

Her father, skeptical until now, asked her for help buying a smartphone with her gaming income. “Is this all from... playing?” he asked, eyebrows raised.

She nodded.

By 2030, Riya wasn’t just playing Axie anymore. She had moved on to other P2E (Play-to-Earn) titles:

- **Star Atlas**, where she mined resources and traded them.
- **Illuvium**, where she captured rare creatures and sold them as NFTs.
- **Zed Run**, where she owned digital horses and entered races for prize money.

She also started coaching beginners, charging small crypto fees for training sessions. Her once-dismissed “hobby” had turned into a full-time job—complete with income, global community, and self-respect.

The beauty of the Metaverse was this: it didn’t care about your gender, your city, or your background. If you had a phone and passion, the doors were open.

By the time she turned 21, Riya had saved enough to renovate her home. She gifted her brother a laptop and taught him how to play responsibly. And yes, her father now proudly told neighbors, “My daughter is a professional gamer.”

Play2Earn = (3 hrs/day × ₹200/game average) × 30 days = ₹18,000/month

REAL JOBS IN A VIRTUAL WORLD — THE NEW CAREER PATHS OF THE METAVERSE

It was 7:45 AM in Pune, and Aryan had already "reached office." But there was no traffic. No cab. No commute. Just a quiet corner in his apartment, a laptop, and his VR headset.

His company? A Metaverse startup based in Amsterdam.

His role? Community Manager.

Every morning, Aryan logged into Spatial — a 3D virtual workspace — where his job was to engage with the global users of their NFT project. He organized virtual events, hosted Q&A sessions inside Metaverse amphitheaters, moderated Discord chats, and helped users set up their crypto wallets. He was earning in USDC — a stablecoin — and getting paid more than most freshers in traditional marketing roles.

Just five years ago, Aryan had no idea this career even existed. He was studying communication and volunteering at college events. When he first heard about the Metaverse, he thought it was just gaming. But then he discovered something amazing — behind every successful Metaverse project was a team. A real team. With real jobs.

From developers who wrote smart contracts, to artists who built 3D assets... From marketers who created NFT launches, to tech support agents helping users navigate virtual spaces — there was a full industry forming.

Aryan's best friend, Meera, had gone down a different path. She was a Metaverse tour guide.

Yes, that's right — a virtual tour guide.

Every week, she guided first-time users through the landscapes of The Sandbox and Decentraland. She showed them where to find events, buy NFT wearables, explore art galleries, and even attend live music shows. For each tour, she earned tips — sometimes in MATIC, sometimes in ETH.

"It's like being a mix of a travel agent, YouTuber, and community helper," she'd say with a laugh.

And then there was Piyush — the silent coder in the group. He wasn't much for talking, but he could build smart contracts in his sleep. He created NFT minting platforms for artists, audited Metaverse codebases, and wrote backend systems for decentralized games. All this from a small village in Madhya Pradesh.

The most beautiful part?

None of them had left India.

Yet all of them were working in global teams, earning global currencies, and building the future of work — all from their own homes.

The Metaverse wasn't some distant dream. It was a live, breathing space with offices, deadlines, and teamwork — just like any traditional job, except without the rigid rules.

People had started asking new questions:

- "Where do you *log in* to work?"
- "What wallet do you get *paid* in?"
- "Which DAO do you contribute to?"

These were the new watercooler conversations.

And as thousands of Indians joined this workforce, the Metaverse became not just a playground — but a powerful economy.

DIGITAL ART, FASHION & VIRTUAL GOODS — THE CREATORS OF THE METAVERSE

It was a Sunday afternoon in Delhi, and Simran sat with her sketchpad—not to draw on paper, but to scan her new NFT collection into her laptop. She wasn't your typical artist. She didn't do gallery shows or sell paintings at exhibitions. Simran was a Metaverse fashion designer.

In this new world, her models were avatars. Her dresses were digital files. And her customers were spread across the globe—people who wore her NFT outfits to parties inside Decentraland or Roblox social events.

“I used to love sketching bridal outfits,” Simran said. “Now I’m designing holographic capes, digital saris, and neon hoodies for avatars.”

Her work was sold on NFT marketplaces like OpenSea and Rarible. One virtual lehenga fetched her ₹40,000—in Ethereum. Not bad for something that didn’t physically exist.

But Simran wasn’t alone.

India had quietly become a hub of digital creators. Artists from Jaipur, Kerala, and Goa were showcasing their 3D artworks, animations, and audio-visual NFTs in virtual galleries. Their fans? Spread across the U.S., Japan, the UAE, and Europe. No visa needed. Just creativity.

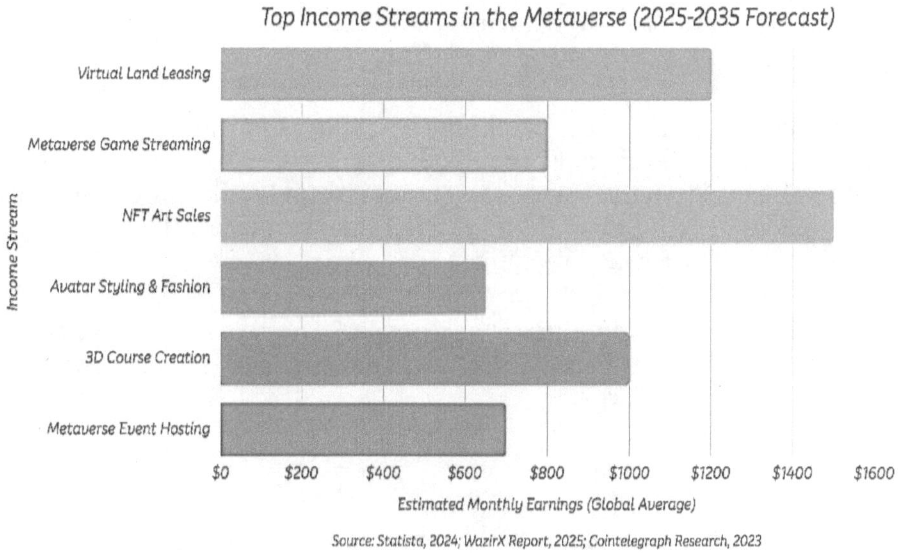

Take *Arjun*, for instance, a young animation student from Kochi. He built a 3D museum in The Sandbox where his animated short films played in loop. He charged an entry fee—₹100 in MATIC—to access the experience.

There was also *Nikita*, a self-taught 3D artist from Gujarat who made wearable accessories—glasses, shoes, earrings—for avatars. Once, she sold a pair of cyberpunk-themed heels as NFTs for 0.8 ETH (around ₹1.5 lakhs at the time). And she continues to earn royalties each time someone resells them.

Brands were quick to notice this creator economy.

Gucci, Nike, and Dolce & Gabbana launched digital collections. Virtual sneakers. NFT handbags. Branded avatar skins. And who helped them design it? Not just big agencies, but also young freelancers from India with laptops and bold ideas.

Even traditional influencers began shifting.

A social media influencer named *Tanvi* from Mumbai started styling avatars. Her Instagram used to be full of fashion selfies. Now? It showed her virtual lookbooks – outfits she created for followers who wanted to look cool at Metaverse meetups. She styled avatars the same way stylists dress celebrities. And yes, she got paid – in USDC.

Fashion schools were catching up too. Institutes in Delhi, Bengaluru, and Kolkata were introducing Metaverse fashion design as a subject. Students learned to create virtual textiles, test them in 3D spaces, and upload them to NFT marketplaces. The runway wasn't in Paris. It was on-chain.

Digital goods were no longer "just pixels." They were identity. Just like we wear clothes in real life to express ourselves, people now did the same in virtual worlds.

The psychology was simple:

- ❖ A new avatar skin was like buying a cool outfit.
- ❖ A rare NFT was like owning a luxury watch.
- ❖ A custom emote was like having your own dance move.

And creators? They weren't starving artists anymore. They were digital entrepreneurs with global customers, instant payments, and complete control over their art.

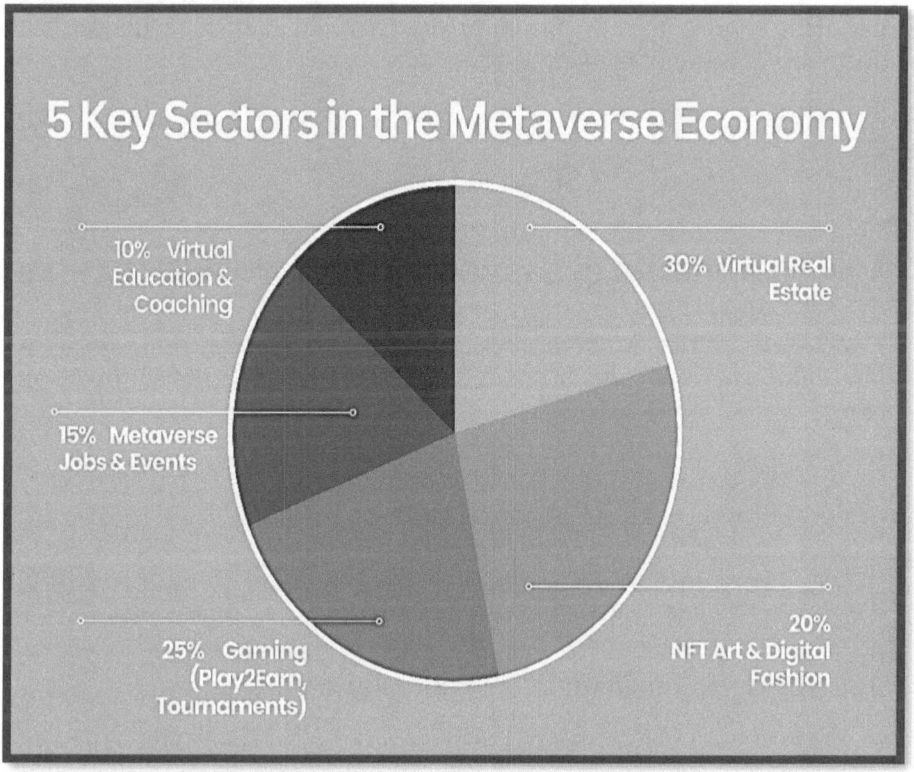

In the Metaverse, art was not limited by walls, borders, or galleries. It floated in air, lived in code, and danced in pixels.

And for thousands of Indians, it became the first step toward global fame—and financial freedom

EDUCATION & LEARNING IN THE METAVERSE — A NEW CLASSROOM WITHOUT WALLS

In a small village near Pune, a teenage boy named Aarav sits at a desk. But instead of staring at a blackboard or textbook, he wears a lightweight VR headset. He isn't just watching a video lesson – he's standing inside a virtual science lab, watching atoms spin around him. His biology teacher, Priya ma'am, appears as a friendly avatar, guiding him through DNA structures.

Aarav isn't a student at a big-city school. His family doesn't own a car. His school barely has a proper science lab. But inside the Metaverse, none of those matters.

Because here, he's in the front row — always.

A WORLD WHERE CLASSROOMS HAVE NO BOUNDARIES

Education in the Metaverse is not limited by location, fees, or language. Anyone with a basic device and an internet connection can:

- Walk through virtual classrooms.
- Interact with AI-powered tutors.
- Conduct science experiments.
- Learn history by walking through ancient Rome or visiting the Taj Mahal as it stood centuries ago.

And this is not imagination — it's already happening.

Indian platforms like NextMeet, Eduversity, and Bodh VR are building Metaverse-based learning tools where:

- Teachers teach as avatars.
- Students participate in real-time.
- Exams are conducted using blockchain for transparency.
- Certificates are issued as NFTs — tamper-proof and globally accepted.

In Hyderabad, Neha, a retired math teacher, now conducts weekend VR classes for kids across India. She teaches geometry inside a 3D world where children build pyramids and shapes with their hands using motion sensors. Neha earns in USDT and receives tips from parents abroad — something unimaginable just a decade ago.

In Kolkata, Imran, a UPSC aspirant, attends a virtual current affairs seminar every Sunday hosted in Spatial. Guest speakers log in from Delhi, Singapore, and New York. The experience? As immersive as a real auditorium.

Even competitive coaching has entered the Metaverse. Platforms now offer IIT-JEE, NEET, and CA prep in gamified 3D settings where students solve puzzles, interact with AI bots, and **earn** crypto rewards for consistency.

Metaverse Opportunity = Skill × Wi-Fi × Time × Global Reach

(No degree, no gatekeepers, no geography limits)

TEACHERS BECOME CREATORS

In the traditional system, a teacher earns a monthly salary and has limited reach.

In the Metaverse:

- They create their own 3D classrooms.
- Record immersive lessons once.
- Upload it to a marketplace like ClassVerse or LearnChain.
- Get paid every time a student views, downloads, or subscribes.

Teachers now have global students and crypto incomes.

Some are even partnering with designers to make learning beautiful. Imagine a physics teacher collaborating with a Metaverse architect to build a floating classroom shaped like a space station. Or a literature teacher walking students through a virtual forest while reciting Rabindranath Tagore's poems.

LEARNING BY DOING

The best part? Education isn't just about reading anymore – it's about doing.

Want to learn architecture? Build real-time models on a 3D site.
Want to study medicine? Step into a human body and zoom into cells.
Want to explore space? Travel through a virtual solar system, dodging asteroids as you learn.

This isn't science fiction. These are daily lessons in some of the world's top Metaverse universities.

Even Harvard, MIT, and Oxford are experimenting with blockchain-based degrees and virtual classrooms.

And India? India is catching up fast.

PAY, CERTIFY, AND PROGRESS — ALL DIGITALLY

Students who complete Metaverse courses receive:

- NFT-based certificates.
- Blockchain-verified transcripts.
- Portfolio tokens that showcase all the projects they've done.

And yes, companies are hiring based on these credentials.

A student from Nagpur who built a weather app inside Roblox was recently hired by a US-based Web3 startup – all because his NFT portfolio proved his skills.

Many ed-tech platforms are now launching “earn while you learn” models, where:

- Students earn tokens for attendance, assignments, and consistency.
- Tokens can be redeemed for merchandise, new courses, or even internships.
- Progress is tracked transparently on-chain.

EDUCATION THAT PAYS THE BILLS

For some students, the Metaverse has even replaced part-time jobs.

A 16-year-old girl from Assam named *Manju* runs a “Homework Help Booth” in a Roblox-based campus. She helps younger students understand math basics using digital games — and charges 10 MATIC per session.

Her story is not unique. Students across India now:

- Tutor in VR classrooms.
- Host webinars in digital amphitheaters.
- Sell mini-courses as NFTs.
- Teach dance, coding, music, and yoga inside 3D studios.

Their clients? From the U.S. to Africa.

Their earnings? In crypto — global, instant, and often higher than traditional jobs.

THE CHALLENGES? YES, THEY EXIST.

The Metaverse isn’t perfect.

Not everyone has a stable internet connection. Not every school has funds for devices. And not every teacher is trained for immersive tools.

But just like smartphones and online classes slowly entered rural India, the Metaverse will too.

Startups are building low-bandwidth VR platforms. Governments are exploring digital scholarship programs. And creators are designing Metaverse classrooms that run on smartphones.

Because the benefits are too powerful to ignore.

At the heart of it all, education in the Metaverse gives something traditional systems rarely offer — freedom.

Freedom to learn what you love.
Freedom to teach from anywhere.
Freedom to grow at your own pace.
And freedom to earn while you learn.

How To Enter the Borderless Metaverse Economy

Skill or Interest

↓

Choose Metaverse Domain (Art, Gaming, Education, Services)

↓

Create a Digital Identity (Avatar, Profile, Wallet)

↓

Join a Platform (Decentraland, Spatial, Sandbox, Roblox, etc.)

↓

Engage → Offer → Earn (NFT, Crypto, Stablecoin)

↓

Withdraw or Reinvest → Grow Your Digital Assets

WILL THE METAVERSE REPLACE THE REAL WORLD?

Shimla, 2035,

The cold breeze touched Rhea's face as she sat on her balcony with a warm cup of chai. The mountains were silent, the snow sparkled, and the world outside was peaceful. But inside her house, something amazing had just happened.

Rhea had just finished hosting a big event. It wasn't in Delhi or Mumbai. It wasn't even in India. It was in the *Metaverse* — a floating digital auditorium, surrounded by virtual waterfalls and glowing lights.

People from around the world had joined. Some were from Japan, some from Kenya, and some from the US. They sat together as avatars, clapping, reacting, asking questions. Rhea had spoken on the environment — a topic close to her heart — and earned tips from attendees, all in crypto.

As she sat back and looked at the mountains, one question came to her mind:

"Is this the future? Will the Metaverse take over everything?"

The Simple Answer: Not Everything Will Change.

No, the real world is not going anywhere.

People will always enjoy going out, traveling, eating at roadside stalls, dancing at weddings, hugging their parents, and walking barefoot on wet grass. These are the joys of real life.

But the Metaverse? It adds something new.
Something exciting.
Something powerful.

It doesn't replace the real world.
It expands it.

TWO WORLDS, ONE LIFE

In 2035, most people live in two worlds — one real, one virtual. They wake up, brush their teeth, make breakfast, help their kids get ready for school. But after that? They put on their VR headset or open their Metaverse app and enter a whole new space.

In that world:

- They attend office meetings in floating glass towers.
- They sell digital clothes to avatars from Brazil or South Korea.
- They teach classes to students from five different countries—all from their homes in Lucknow or Pune.

Real earnings. Real work. Real dreams.

But when the work is done, they still go out for a walk. They still meet friends for coffee. They still attend weddings and family functions.

It's not "either this or that."

It's both.

A NEW KIND OF WORK LIFE

Aarav, a game designer from Jaipur, works for a gaming company based in the Netherlands. His team includes people from Italy, South Africa, and Thailand. But none of them have ever met in person.

They meet in a virtual office every day. They share ideas, build games, and laugh together—just like in a real office. The only difference?

- Aarav doesn't need to spend time in traffic.
- He doesn't need a visa to work for a foreign company.

- He doesn't need to wear formals (unless his avatar wants to).

His salary is paid in Ethereum, and he pays his rent using stablecoins. But every evening, he still walks his dog, has dinner with his parents, and goes out for street food on weekends.

The Metaverse gave him a career.

But the real world still gives him joy.

WEARING DIGITAL CLOTHES IN A REAL-LIFE WORLD

Imagine buying a new kurta—but not for yourself, for your avatar.

In the Metaverse, fashion has gone fully digital. Top brands like Gucci, Nike, and even Indian designers now create NFT clothing that people buy, wear, and show off inside virtual worlds.

Fashion students in India have become Metaverse stylists. They design clothes, shoes, and jewelry for avatars. These are sold like limited-edition collectibles—and some sell for lakhs of rupees!

But does that mean people stopped buying real clothes?

Of course not.

People still dress up for weddings, photoshoots, or just to feel good. But now, they also dress up their digital selves—especially when their work, social life, and hobbies also exist online.

The Metaverse didn't stop fashion.

It gave it another stage.

CONCERTS, CLASSES, AND CONFERENCES — WITHOUT LEAVING HOME

In 2035, a 16-year-old girl in Guwahati can attend a live concert by a Brazilian singer, sitting in her room with a headset.

A retired teacher in Kochi can host a lecture for students from the UK and Kenya—inside a VR classroom.

A college student in Punjab can watch a business conference, network with CEOs, and pitch his startup idea, all without stepping out of his room.

These events feel real.
Because they are real.

You pay real money for tickets. You meet real people. You learn real things. The only difference is—you don't need to travel, book hotels, or get visas.

And the best part? When it ends, you're already home.

IT'S NOT SCIENCE FICTION — IT'S ALREADY HERE

When Facebook changed its name to Meta, the world took notice. But Indians were already building, learning, and earning in the Metaverse.

Fashion brands, gaming companies, colleges, artists, musicians, startups — they all joined the new economy.

Artists from Rajasthan opened NFT art galleries. Developers from Chennai worked for Metaverse platforms. Fashion designers in Delhi sold digital sarees.

India didn't just join the Metaverse.

India helped shape it.

REAL WORLD STILL MATTERS

The Metaverse has added new options. But it hasn't taken away what matters.

People still:

- Travel to Goa for a vacation.
- Stand in long lines at temples.
- Eat hot samosas from street vendors.
- Feel the touch of rain on their skin.

No VR headset can copy those feelings.

And truthfully? It shouldn't try to.

Because the goal of the Metaverse isn't to replace.

The goal is to enhance.

To give more people more access.

To let a student in a village study at an international school.

To let a young artist earn money from a global audience.

To let a mother work from home and still attend office meetings in a virtual boardroom.

FINAL THOUGHT: A BLENDED FUTURE

Rhea looked at the snow again. Her chai had gone cold, but her heart felt warm.

She didn’t need to choose between the real world and the digital one.
She could live in both.

She could host global events and cook dinner with her mother.
She could walk through virtual cities and hike real mountains.

That’s what the Metaverse really is—
Not a replacement.
But a new layer on top of life.

A place where dreams stretch further.
Where geography doesn't matter.
Where anyone, from anywhere, can shine.

And as India leads this revolution, one click, one course, one creative step at a time.

It becomes clear:

We’re not escaping reality.

We’re building more of it.

> *“The metaverse removes the one border no one talks about—opportunity. Now a villager in Assam from India and a coder in New York can work in the same room.”*
>
> *— Inspired by Vitalik Buterin & Metaverse Visionaries*

*****

"The next wave of technology isn't about devices—it's about intelligence and trust. AI and blockchain are the foundation."

©Satya Nadella (Microsoft CEO)

CHAPTER SIX

AI, BLOCKCHAIN & THE NEXT WAVE OF DECENTRALIZATION

"The convergence of AI and blockchain is not just a technological shift—it's the beginning of a new civilization layer."

– Balaji Srinivasan, former CTO of Coinbase, angel investor, and author of The Network State

---

Bangalore, 2035,

The morning light cuts through the glass towers of Bangalore, now glowing not just with sunshine—but with data. The city's pulse is no longer traffic or coffee-fueled hustle. It's blockchain. It's artificial intelligence. It's decentralized everything.

And walking calmly through the neon-lit streets of what was once called HITEC City is Anjan.

But this isn't the HITEC City his parents knew. The crowded cubicles, long queues for swipe-ins, and Monday blues are gone. In their place stand glassy, silent, self-driving co-working hubs that recognize you before you enter.

As Anjan steps into the building, he doesn't reach for a keycard or even open his laptop. His smart glasses blink to life, and within seconds, everything is ready—his workspace, his codebase, his analytics dashboard, and even a steaming hot cup of masala tea waiting on the smart desk.

No passwords. No logins. No waiting.

All of it triggered by his AI assistant—a sentient digital companion he coded himself, powered by a decentralized blockchain network that ensures no tech giant can own or spy on it.

This is not some futuristic dream.
This is a regular Tuesday in Anjan's world.

THE STARTUP THAT DOESN'T SLEEP

Anjan runs a blockchain-powered AI firm. But here's the twist: his company doesn't have a traditional team, a big office, or even a bank account.

It runs on smart contracts.
It breathes through decentralized protocols.
It sleeps never.

Every part of the company is powered by code:

- Smart contracts pay contributors instantly once a task is done.

- ❖ The AI negotiates client deals by studying real-time market conditions.

- ❖ All data is stored in a decentralized cloud—safe, encrypted, and far from government or corporate control.

He once joked with a friend, "My startup works harder than I do... and never takes weekends off."

But the truth is, Anjan doesn't feel like he's working anymore. He feels like he's playing with the future.

And winning.

A NEW KIND OF OFFICE, A NEW KIND OF FREEDOM

Remember the old days of 9-to-5?

Anjan doesn't.

Because he doesn't need a boss.

He doesn't need HR, payroll teams, or middle managers. His entire company is a mix of AI agents, blockchain tools, and contributors from across the world—paid in crypto, working in the Metaverse.

Some days, he logs in from his co-working pod.
Other days, from a beach house in Gokarna.
Once, even from a tent in Ladakh.

Work follows him—not the other way around.

What People Once Feared, Became the Future We Needed.

Anjan remembers the stories his parents told him.

Back in 2020s, people feared that AI would steal their jobs.
That automation would end careers.
That blockchain was just hype.

But here he is in 2035—living proof that they were wrong.

AI didn't replace humans.

It freed them.

Blockchain didn't destroy industries. It rebuilt them. Together, they created something better—a new world of work where no one had to rely on slow banks, greedy corporations, or outdated rules.

People began to own their work. Their time. Their worth.

That was the real revolution.

The Office with No Boss, No Borders

At 2 PM, Anjan's AI pings him: "New proposal from a biotech DAO in Brazil. Should I review it?"

He nods, and the AI starts negotiating terms in the background.

By 2:15 PM, a smart contract is drafted.

By 2:17 PM, the deal is signed—no Zoom calls, no paperwork, no timezone struggles.

This is what work looks like in 2035.

Borderless. Paperless. Permissionless.

You don't apply for jobs—you contribute to networks. You don't beg for salaries—you earn instantly through smart

contracts.
You don't work for a company—you *are* the company.

It's a world where your skill is your passport, and the blockchain is your resume.

From Dependency to Digital Power

When Anjan finishes his day, there are no emails waiting. No stress. No traffic jam to survive.

He leans back, takes off his glasses, and watches the Bangalore skyline—a mix of digital and physical worlds blending into something beautiful.

He thinks of how much has changed.

Two decades ago:

- You needed a bank to start a business.
- You needed a visa to work abroad.
- You needed a manager's approval for everything.

Now?

- Your wallet is your identity.
- Your skill speaks louder than your degree.
- Your work earns while you sleep.

This isn't just a shift in technology.

It's a shift in *power*.

Power is no longer in the hands of the few.
It's in the hands of those who build, create, and own—digitally. And Anjan? He's not just part of it.

He's one of the builders of this new world.

This Is Just the Beginning.

As the evening lights dance on his smart desk, Anjan gets a message from a 17-year-old coder in Jaipur.

"Can I contribute to your AI project? I've built a sentiment engine that runs on-chain."

Anjan smiles. That was him, a few years ago. Curious. Fearless. Ready to build without waiting for permission.

He types back:
"Sure. Fork the repo. If it works, the contract will pay you instantly."

No interviews. No gatekeeping. No glass ceilings.

Just raw talent. Real opportunity. Total freedom.

This, right here, is what the Metaverse Economy + AI + Blockchain has given the world.

Not just cooler tech.
Not just fancier tools.
But a future where anyone can rise.

No matter who you are.
No matter where you live.

THE INTERSECTION OF AI & BLOCKCHAIN — A NEW DIGITAL ECONOMY

On a warm afternoon in Chennai, Priya listened as her AI assistant chirped, "Your health summary is ready." Moments later, her smart glasses displayed a visual of her daily biomarkers—heart rate, sleep pattern, stress level—calculated using AI models updated in real time. What Priya couldn't see was the powerful force behind the screen: blockchain.

Every data point—heartbeats, steps, calories burned—was securely recorded on a decentralized ledger. The result? Priya trusted her health statistics, knowing no one could manipulate or delete them. This fusion of **AI analysis** and **blockchain trust** was quietly reshaping lives—making cities smarter, industries fairer, and economies more transparent.

WHY THIS COMBINATION MATTERS

Both AI and blockchain are powerful tools on their own. But together? They create something revolutionary.

- **Blockchain** brings decentralization, transparency, and security.
- **AI** brings automation, intelligence, and lightning-fast decision-making.

Individually, each sparks discussion. But when merged, they pave the way for a new digital economy—built not on hidden algorithms or gatekeepers, but on trust and intelligent automation.

AI Makes Decisions, Blockchain Makes Them Trustworthy

Every day, AI systems analyze mountains of data: financial trends, production statistics, personal behavior. AI can spot patterns, predict outcomes, and make decisions—instantly.

But the question always arises: *Can we trust AI?*

Transparency and accountability are rare in traditional systems. Even professionals struggle to verify why certain decisions were made.

Blockchain changes that.

Imagine a smart contract that uses AI to assess loan applications. The AI runs its calculations, evaluating credit history, income, and repayment ability. The blockchain records both the inputs (loan data) and the decision (approved or rejected), timestamped and immutable.

Later, if someone questions the decision, everything is transparent and auditable. No shady bias, no hidden model quirks—just clear logic captured on-chain.

In industries like finance and healthcare, this isn't just nice—it's necessary for trust.

AI Learns from Data, Blockchain Protects It

AI systems need vast, high-quality data to learn and improve. From training chatbots to predicting market shifts, the value of AI depends on the data it consumes.

But data is fragile.

It can be hacked. It can be altered. It can vanish.

Here's where blockchain steps in.

By storing or verifying critical data on-chain, blockchain ensures that once data lands on the ledger, it cannot be modified. This keeps AI's learning datasets secure, fair, and authentic.

Take the example of a Mumbai hospital network using AI to detect early-stage diseases. With blockchain protection, patient data isn't altered. Patient history stays intact. Doctors evolve trust in the AI's predictions.

That trust improves patient care—and builds user confidence in the system at scale.

AI + Blockchain = Autonomous Trust Infrastructure

AI Automates and Blockchain Ensures Fair Execution

In the Metaverse world we're building, automation happens everywhere:

- AI negotiates contract terms
- AI executes trades
- AI flags fraud

Small errors or biases in these tasks can mean big losses or injustice.

With blockchain, each step is stamped and secure.

Imagine an AI system that buys energy credits for a smart city. It monitors usage, smartly decides when to buy and sell, and logs each transaction using a blockchain-backed smart contract. No middleman. No delay. No tampering.

If something goes wrong—a bug, wrong data—the event is traceable with full clarity.

In digital economies, security isn't just about encryption. It's about transparency and accountability—and AI plus blockchain delivers it.

HOW AI & BLOCKCHAIN COMPLEMENT EACH OTHER

Function	**AI Does**	**Blockchain Ensures**
Data Analysis	Reads and interprets large datasets in real time	Immutable and auditable data storage

Decision Making	Automates smart decisions using ML/Neural Networks	Transparent execution using smart contracts
Identity Verification	Facial recognition, behavioral patterns	Self-sovereign digital identity (DID)
Transactions & Payments	Fraud detection, real-time settlement	Trustless, peer-to-peer validation
Resource Allocation	Optimizes resources and predicts needs	Prevents tampering and ensures fair execution

REAL-WORLD EXAMPLES AT WORK

Let's visit a few places where this partnership is already changing industries:

SMART FARMS IN GUJARAT

In fields just outside Ahmedabad, farmers no longer rely on guesswork. Instead, they deploy AI drones that hover over the crops at dawn. These drones capture images of wheat and onion fields, scanning them for signs of disease, pest infestations, or water stress. In a matter of minutes, the AI analyzes its data—identifying tiny yellowing leaves or fungal spots no human eye might catch.

Here's where blockchain becomes crucial: every analysis point, every alert, is recorded on a decentralized ledger. That means once the data enters the system, it can't be tampered with. No one can hide evidence of disease or falsify yield estimates.

At harvest time, small-scale and larger buyers can scan a QR code on the packed produce. Instantly, they know exactly what they're getting: "Harvested on October 5, inspected via drone on October 1, disease-free." This level of traceability and trust boosts the farm's reputation and allows farmers to earn premium prices.

For the first time, rural farmers stand side by side with large agribusinesses—able to show real, verified data to global buyers. AI powers insights; blockchain guarantees trust.

SECURE HEALTH RECORDS IN KOCHI

In Kochi's serene tech zone, a small hospital group rolled out a cutting-edge digital health project. Patients wear smart bands that track everything—heart rate, sleep quality, glucose levels. The AI instantly categorizes patterns: a worrying drop in oxygen levels, or an unusual spike in temperature.

But this isn't all done in a private silo. Each new health datapoint is encrypted and stored on-chain, accessible only by the patient and authorized practitioners. The moment a doctor checks a record; the access is logged transparently—protecting both privacy and accountability.

A breakthrough happened one day when the AI detected early signs of heat stress in a patient. A smart contract automatically triggered a mild treatment plan: it booked the next available lab appointment, adjusted the patient's diet recommendations, and sent reminders via text—all without human delay.

That saved time. It saved money. It saved worry.

The hospital, now known for proactive care, attracts patients from nearby towns. Even aligned with public health efforts, this AI-blockchain combo has enabled digital trust in a field where trust is life.

DECENTRALIZED DIGITAL IDENTITY IN HYDERABAD

In India's cyber hub of Hyderabad, residents once faced long waits for simple tasks—applying for driver's licenses, bank accounts, or public service benefits. Paperwork piled up. Systems rarely spoke to each other. Lost documents meant lost time.

Today, citizens carry crypto-wallet-based IDs instead. When Sahil moves to a new city, he no longer needs physical address proofs. He simply proves his identity using blockchain—where records of residency, identity, and credentials are stored and verified via his encrypted ID.

When he applies for a supermarket loyalty card or a government subsidy, AI verifies his eligibility conditions instantly. The application and verification become fast—even real-time. When access is granted, it's logged in a smart contract. Sahil receives his benefit—maybe a subsidy for solar panels—within seconds, as crypto tokens sent to his wallet.

No visits. No paper documents. No long lines.

And each step? Fully recorded, fully transparent, fully controlled by Sahil himself.

SEAMLESS TRAVEL INSURANCE IN BENGALURU

Meet Kavya, a frequent flyer and startup founder from Bengaluru. She purchases travel insurance using a decentralized app. The policy—written as a smart contract—automatically activates the moment her flight is registered.

On the day of travel, Kavya's flight gets delayed. Now, she doesn't call the insurer. AI feeds real-time flight data to the smart contract. Blockchain confirms the delay. Instantly, the policy executes and releases compensation—directly to her wallet in stablecoins.

In the old system, she'd have waited days, submitted forms, or argued with agents. Instead, she gets peace of mind and pizza delivery cash—all before stepping out of the airport lounge.

This union of AI and blockchain creates a travel experience where everything happens quietly behind the scenes, leaving Kavya to do what really matters.

FRACTIONAL REAL ESTATE IN PUNE

In Pune's emerging digital economy, there's a new way to buy property. Not entire homes—but small, fractional shares—like buying a piece of your favorite painting.

Real estate agencies use AI to track property values across city zones. When they spot a trending neighborhood, they tokenize a building on the blockchain—dividing it into shares anyone can buy, trade, or hold.

Look at Priya, a tech professional. She bought 5% of a tech-office built through tokenized real estate. AI calculates her daily rent share from tenant activity. Smart contracts distribute rental payouts automatically to her wallet. She watches her investment grow—all without meetings, agents, or hidden fees.

When she wants, she sells her share to someone eyeing Pune's growing tech corridor. Transaction complete, on-chain, and transparent.

Everyone gains—developers get early funding; buyers get flexibility; and the real estate market becomes liquid, affordable, and instantly connected.

WHAT THESE STORIES TEACH US

Each of these use cases shows a similar pattern:

- **Smart Insights**: AI studies real-world events—from crop health to flight delays—to act fast or learn.
- **Tamper-Proof Recording**: Blockchain ensures all data and actions are secure, transparent, and traceable.
- **Autonomous Action**: Smart contracts execute decisions—subsidy, payout, update—without middlemen.
- **Trust Through Transparency**: When people trust the system, participation grows—and innovation spreads.

This isn't about replacing human effort. It's about amplifying trust and eliminating friction in daily lives.

The real magic here isn't just technology. It's what that technology enables:

- A farmer in Gujarat who gains trust—and better prices.
- A patient in Kochi who gets cared for faster—and with dignity.
- A citizen in Hyderabad who becomes a digital citizen—fully empowered.
- A traveler in Bengaluru who gets fair insurance—without paperwork.
- An everyday investor in Pune who finds a smarter way to grow wealth.

These real-world stories highlight what many only talk about:

"A digital economy built not just on speed and scale—but on fairness, transparency, and trust."

Where intelligent systems make decisions, and decentralized platforms ensure those decisions are real and safe. Where people anywhere—whether in a village, suburb, or metro—can benefit and grow.

BEYOND TECH: A FAIRER FUTURE

In the old world, your fate could be shaped by paperwork, gatekeepers, or hidden bias.

In this new age, if you work honestly, your actions matter. If you deserve a loan, the system shows why. If you deserve payouts, the contracts execute themselves. If you deserve opportunities, AI can present them—free of prejudice.

It's a world where:

- ❖ People from small towns can get loans as fast as those in metros.
- ❖ Industries can track raw materials from farm to factory without fraud.
- ❖ Citizens can access government services online without bribes or delay.
- ❖ Students can validate achievements and skill credentials instantly.

The partnership between Artificial Intelligence and Blockchain is like the meeting of mind and memory—one thinks, the other remembers. Together, they're creating a system that doesn't just operate automatically... it operates *intelligently and transparently*. But like all powerful ideas, this one is still in its early chapters.

AI is evolving fast—but it still has lessons to learn. How to make fair decisions. How to filter out bias hidden in data. How to serve everyone, not just the privileged. Meanwhile, blockchain—known for its transparency and security—is trying to scale up. It's learning how to carry heavier loads of information, how to interact with AI in real-time, and how to make trust digital on a global scale.

The technology is moving faster than the rules. In most parts of the world, including India, regulations are still catching up. So is education. But innovation rarely waits.

Today, in cities like Hyderabad, Mumbai, and Bengaluru, something exciting is happening. These aren't just tech hubs anymore. They're becoming the launchpads of a decentralized, AI-powered future. Startups are receiving grants to explore AI-governed contracts. Government-backed pilot programs are testing blockchain in voting, education, and agriculture. And inside universities, students and researchers are coding the next breakthroughs in autonomous finance, smart cities, and digital identity.

But perhaps most exciting of all? You don't need to be an expert to join this wave. In cafés, coworking spaces, and online forums across India, a new generation of creators, coders, dreamers, and builders is rising. They're not just waiting for the future—they're building it. With code, curiosity, and conviction.

This isn't just a tech trend. It's a transformation. And in India, the seeds of that transformation are already in bloom.

THE BIG PICTURE

Imagine waking up in a world where your daily life runs smoother—not because of more apps, but because of smarter systems working together behind the scenes. Your smart fridge, noticing you're low on milk and vegetables, sends out an automated order. But it doesn't use a food delivery app. It talks directly to local vendors via AI-powered smart contracts.

These contracts instantly check availability, compare prices, and lock in the best deal. No human middleman. No unnecessary calls. Once the delivery is confirmed at your doorstep, the blockchain logs it in real time—verifiable, unchangeable, and timestamped.

The farmers who supplied those vegetables? They receive instant payment in stablecoins like USDC or Digital Rupees, directly into their blockchain wallets. No delays. No banks. No hidden fees. It's honest, automatic, and fair.

And you? You don't even touch your phone. The payment happens through your linked digital wallet, managed by your home AI assistant, ensuring every transaction is both secure and budget-friendly.

This isn't a sci-fi dream. This is the bigger picture—the real-world magic that happens when AI, blockchain, and decentralized finance unite. A seamless, borderless, trustless economy where everything just... works.

No red tape. No broken systems. Just pure flow.

Blockchain and AI aren't just technologies.
They're co-pilots in the next evolution of our lives.
They're unlocking a digital economy that is smarter, fairer, and open to everyone.

And it all started when two giants stopped working alone—and began working together.

HOW AI & BLOCKCHAIN ARE TRANSFORMING INDUSTRIES

AI and blockchain together are reshaping industries by blending intelligence with trust. AI brings speed, automation, and smart decision-making, while blockchain ensures transparency, security, and tamper-proof records. In finance, AI-powered DeFi platforms offer instant loans without paperwork. In healthcare, AI analyzes blockchain-stored records for early diagnosis. In law, smart contracts replace lengthy legal processes. From agriculture to logistics, this powerful duo removes middlemen, reduces fraud, and empowers individuals. India's tech hubs are already building this future—where industries are not just digital, but decentralized and intelligent. This is not just innovation—it's a new way of working, living, and growing.

DECENTRALIZED AI FINANCE (DEFI 2.0)

Dawn in Lucknow,

The early sun painted Sarita's mustard field in soft gold. A gentle breeze carried the scent of wet earth into her open window as she sat on her cot, smartphone in hand.

The notification read:
"₹50,000 microloan available. Approve?"

Sarita tapped "Yes." Within seconds, ₹50,000 landed in her digital wallet. No long queues. No bank visits. No paperwork. Just smart technology working for her.

Behind the scenes, two powerful tools were at work:

- ✓ **ARTIFICIAL INTELLIGENCE (AI)** – gathering and analyzing data: satellite images of her land, soil moisture levels, weather forecasts, and past yields.

- ✓ **BLOCKCHAIN** – securely verifying her land records, encoding loan terms in a smart contract, and recording every step immutably.

That ₹50,000 was more than money. It was freedom and recognition. It acknowledged her effort, her land's potential, and her right to equitable access to finance.

THE MECHANICS: HOW AI + BLOCKCHAIN REDEFINE FINANCE

This quick moment of empowerment reflects a broader shift called DeFi 2.0 – Decentralized AI Finance. Here's how it critiques and transforms traditional banking:

INCLUSIVE, DATA-DRIVEN LENDING

AI reduces bias by evaluating loan requests based on reliable facts—not gender, connections, or documentation gaps. For Sarita, the AI looked at farm data, not her gender.

SECURE DIGITAL OWNERSHIP

Previously, a lost physical deed could derail everything. Now, blockchain holds unbreakable proof of land ownership—timestamped, tamper-proof, always accessible.

AUTOMATED, SMART CONTRACTS

Once Sarita approves the loan, a smart contract executes repayment terms automatically, linked to harvest time or crop revenue. It processes repayment requests and disburses funds independently.

TRANSPARENT RECORD-KEEPING

Every action—loan approval, disbursement, repayment—is logged on-chain. Sarita, lenders, regulators, or her child can audit the history. Scam prevention and trust-building become natural outcomes.

> 🧠 *"Artificial intelligence is only as powerful as the trust it earns. That's where blockchain steps in."*

The next morning, Sarita receives another message:

"Heatwave expected next week. Suggest planting drought-resistant millet? Yields estimate +20%. Would you like to adjust?"

This isn't just convenience—it's precision agriculture powered by a combination of AI's analysis and blockchain's secure record-keeping. Farmers make decisions backed by data, transactions are fair and monitored, and outcomes become consistent.

This integrated system achieves three things:

- ✓ **Empowerment** – Farmers are supported by foresight and fair loans.
- ✓ **Protection** – Contracts ensure no one is disadvantaged.
- ✓ **Sustainability** – Better decisions protect the land—and livelihoods.

SCALING BEYOND LUCKNOW

In a quiet village nestled along the flood-prone plains of Bihar, something remarkable is happening. Sarita, a local farmer, no longer waits in line at a bank or pleads with officials for crop loans. Instead, she uses a DeFi 2.0 app on her smartphone. When rainfall drops below normal, the AI system instantly analyzes the weather data and adjusts her loan terms. No paperwork. No middleman. Just relief, when it matters most.

Hundreds of kilometers away in Maharashtra's scenic vineyards, wine growers receive real-time disease forecasts. When AI detects a possible outbreak, blockchain-based smart contracts automatically release insurance payouts—within minutes, not months. The delays of traditional systems are gone.

Down south in Karnataka's coconut-growing belts, farmers like Anand are using digital contract templates stored on-chain. With a few taps, he's able to access tools once reserved for big agribusinesses—fair pricing, transparent agreements, and even export logistics.

This is no longer just theory. It's the future of rural India—where AI and blockchain come together to level the playing field. Where modern finance reaches the heart of the fields, and every farmer becomes a participant in the global economy. DeFi 2.0 isn't a luxury here—it's a lifeline.

Tech accelerators in Bengaluru and Hyderabad now fund village teams to localize app features and train farmers. The result? Reduced loan defaults, stronger harvests, and greater confidence among rural communities.

WHY THIS MATTERS: A SYSTEMS VIEW

This isn't just a rural success story—it signals the future of trust-based digital ecosystems:

- ✓ **For Farmers**: Fairer access, timely insights, and financial independence.
- ✓ **For Fintech Startups**: Efficient underwriting, rapid scaling, and lower risk.
- ✓ **For Regulators**: Transparent, auditable systems with reduced fraud.
- ✓ **For Investors**: Better data, scalable ecosystems, and impact-driven returns.

Meanwhile, the combination of AI and blockchain introduces **a** new economic architecture—one where rules are enforced by code, transparency is built-in, and decisions are grounded in evidence, not bias.

The Human Angle: From Borrower to Digital Citizen

Sarita's transformation also mirrors a shift in identity. She's no longer just a "farmer." She's a digital citizen. She owns her financial trail. She learns from data. She uses tools once reserved for large corporations.

Her success inspires others—the village tailor sets up an online storefront using similar methods, the co-operative buys digital insurance via AI-driven contracts. A silent revolution thrives, farm by farm, app by app.

The Marriage of Tech, Trust, and Transformation

AI and blockchain alone are strong. Together, they become **transformational**. They enable financial products that are inclusive, transparent, and resilient—tailored to local conditions and rooted in individual dignity.

What started as a loan offer in her mustard field becomes a mechanism of empowerment and trust. For Sarita—and thousands like her—this is the future made real.

As we move on, imagine this model extending into healthcare, legal systems, art and music, and global freelancing. Then you'll see how **AI + blockchain** aren't just bits of tech—they're the groundwork for a fair, intelligent world.

AI-POWERED HEALTHCARE ON BLOCKCHAIN: A NEW ERA OF MEDICINE

In a quiet corner of Mumbai, inside a modern hospital known more for its AI servers than waiting rooms, something remarkable is happening. Patients no longer carry paper reports or wait for weeks to get results. Instead, they walk in, scan a QR code, and unlock a world of intelligent healthcare powered by two groundbreaking technologies: **Artificial Intelligence (AI)** and **Blockchain**.

The Problem Healthcare Always Had

For decades, the healthcare industry has struggled with fragmentation, inaccuracy, and delays:

- Patient records scattered across hospitals.
- Test results lost in bureaucratic loops.
- Delayed diagnoses due to lack of data access.
- Personal medical data often vulnerable to leaks and misuse.

In a country like India—where millions depend on overloaded public systems—this problem is even more severe. But now, a powerful solution is emerging.

BLOCKCHAIN: THE DIGITAL LOCKER FOR HEALTH DATA

Imagine if every X-ray, blood report, prescription, and consultation note you've ever had could be safely stored in one place. That's what blockchain makes possible.

Blockchain allows medical records to be stored securely, in a tamper-proof system that only the patient controls. Hospitals and doctors can access data only when granted permission—ensuring privacy, security, and transparency.

Every update—like a new test or prescription—is timestamped and added immutably. It's like having a personal health passport that no one can forge, delete, or misuse.

ARTIFICIAL INTELLIGENCE: THE BRAIN BEHIND THE CARE

Now comes AI—the brain of this operation.

AI systems trained on millions of cases can detect patterns, analyze symptoms, predict diseases, and even design personalized treatments. This isn't futuristic speculation—it's already happening.

Hospitals across India are deploying AI-driven diagnostic systems that can:

- ❖ Detect early signs of cancer from scans.
- ❖ Predict potential heart conditions.
- ❖ Suggest medication dosages based on lifestyle and medical history.

❖ Alert doctors about critical changes in real-time.

"A future without human error begins with machine precision – locked on the blockchain."

A REAL-WORLD EXAMPLE: MUMBAI'S SMART HOSPITAL

At a hospital in Mumbai, AI systems scan anonymized health records stored on a blockchain network. One patient's case—a 43-year-old man with mild fatigue—reveals something deeper: early-stage pancreatic cancer. Traditional methods might have missed it for months.

But here, AI spotted it instantly, backed by secure and verified data from the blockchain. The patient starts treatment within days—saving time, cost, and possibly his life

BENEFITS OF AI + BLOCKCHAIN IN HEALTHCARE

In the world of healthcare, the fusion of AI and blockchain is quietly rewriting the rules—making the system smarter, safer, and far more inclusive.

Imagine a future where patients are no longer passive participants but empowered custodians of their own medical records. With blockchain, every piece of data—diagnosis, prescription, or report—is encrypted and securely stored, and only the patient decides who gets access. No more fear of data leaks, unauthorized sharing, or lost records.

AI takes it a step further. It analyzes this data in real time, spotting patterns, flagging risks, and giving doctors instant insights for faster and more accurate diagnoses. It's not just smart—it's life-saving.

In rural India, where doctors are few and hospitals are far, AI-powered telehealth platforms backed by blockchain are bridging the gap. Patients can now access specialist care remotely without worrying about privacy or misinformation.

And as the system becomes more automated, administrative delays and human errors shrink—making healthcare not only faster and smarter, but also more affordable. Less paper, fewer mistakes, and more lives saved.

Together, AI and blockchain are not just improving healthcare—they are redefining it for a country as vast and diverse as India.

This is more than a digital upgrade. It's a shift in control. The patient is no longer a passive subject but the owner of their medical journey.

Doctors, too, benefit. With cleaner, verified data, they can focus on what matters—healing, not paperwork. And in a country like India, where one doctor may see hundreds of patients a day, this can be life-changing.

AI and blockchain are not replacing doctors. They are reimagining the healthcare system to be more inclusive, intelligent, and efficient. They reduce the load on hospitals, make healthcare accessible in remote areas, and protect what matters most—our lives and our data.

The revolution has already begun. And with every QR scan and AI diagnosis, India is taking a bold step toward becoming a global leader in smart healthcare.

THE FUTURE OF LAW — WHERE AI AND BLOCKCHAIN REPLACE PAPERWORK

Delhi, 2035,

Meera and Arjun stood in their new apartment, sunlight pouring through the window as they took a deep breath. No court visits. No stacks of papers. No delays. Yet, everything was legally done—flawlessly.

A few weeks ago, they decided to buy this flat. But instead of going through the slow and confusing traditional process, they used an app powered by AI and blockchain.

In the past, buying property meant visiting government offices, hiring brokers, spending on legal fees, waiting weeks for document verification, and hoping everything was genuine.

But today? It took them less than two hours.

SMART CONTRACTS: THE DIGITAL LAWYERS

The core technology behind Meera and Arjun's smooth transaction is something called a smart contract. It's a piece of code that runs on a blockchain. Just like a traditional contract, it records an agreement between two parties — but it does more. Once the terms are met (like a payment made), it automatically executes the deal.

But who writes these smart contracts? Not lawyers. Not humans. Artificial Intelligence (AI) does.

Modern AI systems are trained to read thousands of legal documents, understand different laws, spot errors, and even recommend better terms. Once the user enters some basic details (like names, property location, and price), the AI creates a perfectly formatted, legally valid smart contract, ready to be stored on the blockchain.

HOW BLOCKCHAIN MAKES IT SAFE AND TRUSTWORTHY

Traditional legal systems involve a lot of trust—you trust the broker to be honest, the lawyer to be accurate, and the paperwork to be genuine.

Blockchain removes the need for trust. It creates a digital record that no one can change.

For example:

- The property's ownership history is stored on blockchain.
- Previous transactions and legal status are visible to both buyer and seller.
- Once a smart contract is signed, it's locked forever. No one can tamper with it.

This prevents land fraud, bribe-based approvals, and forged documents—which are sadly common in many countries, including India.

REAL-WORLD APPLICATION: WHAT'S ALREADY HAPPENING

This isn't just a futuristic dream. Many countries and Indian states are already experimenting with blockchain in real estate and legal systems.

- Telangana and Maharashtra have begun blockchain pilots to store land records, making them tamper-proof.
- Startups in Bengaluru and Pune are working on AI tools that read legal files, detect errors, and draft contracts in seconds.
- Estonia and Dubai have fully digital land registration systems using blockchain.
- Platforms like Propy (globally) and Zupple (India) help execute property deals using smart contracts.

So, when Meera and Arjun used an app to buy their flat, they were not just lucky — they were part of a growing movement.

WHAT IT MEANS FOR THE COMMON PERSON

For the average buyer or seller, this shift means:

- ✓ No more long queues at government offices.
- ✓ No hidden charges or third-party manipulations.
- ✓ No delays waiting for paperwork approvals.
- ✓ 100% clarity on property history and ownership.

And for renters, small business owners, or freelancers — AI-generated smart contracts make short-term agreements easier and safer, without needing to hire a lawyer each time.

For example:

- ❖ A landlord in Chennai can rent an apartment to a tenant in minutes with a smart contract.
- ❖ A freelancer in Jaipur can sign a blockchain contract with a client in Canada — and get paid instantly upon task completion.

DOES THIS MEAN LAWYERS WILL DISAPPEAR?

Not exactly.

While smart contracts are replacing basic legal agreements, complex cases, disputes, and court proceedings still need human lawyers and judges. But what will change is how lawyers work.

Instead of manually checking contracts, they will:

- ❖ Review AI-generated contracts.
- ❖ Work on edge cases that AI can't solve.
- ❖ Focus on creative legal strategy instead of repetitive paperwork.

In fact, lawyers who learn to use these new tools will be more in demand, not less.

The legal industry is often seen as slow to change. But with AI and blockchain coming together, we're witnessing a real transformation.

What used to take weeks now takes minutes. What used to require trust in people now relies on code and cryptography.

For countries like India, where legal backlogs and corruption slow down development, this change is massive. Smart contracts and digital law systems could reduce disputes, prevent fraud, and make legal help affordable for everyone.

Meera and Arjun's experience wasn't a one-time miracle. It's becoming the new normal.

This new system is not just about technology. It's about empowering people – giving them tools to take control of their lives, their deals, and their dreams.

So, the next time you think of lawyers, don't imagine dusty files and courtrooms.

Think of clean code, AI advisors, and trustless transactions on a blockchain.

The courtroom of tomorrow may not have four walls – it might live in your pocket. And the judge? It might just be a line of code.

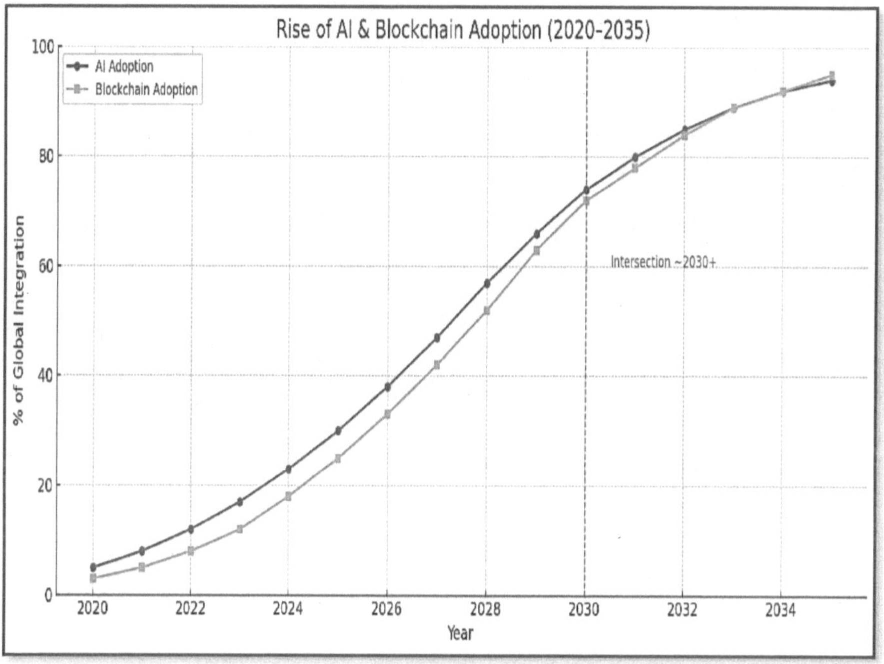

THE NEW STAGE – WHERE AI AND BLOCKCHAIN POWER THE CREATIVE ECONOMY

Kolkata, 2035,

Asha sat on her rooftop, watching the early morning sun rise over the city skyline. She had just received her latest payment—not from a record label or a manager, but directly from her fans across the world.

Her newest Bengali-English fusion song had just gone live—not on Spotify or YouTube, but as an NFT on a decentralized music platform. Within hours, it had sold out. People from Japan, Canada, and Nigeria had bought her track, not just to listen but to own a piece of her music.

There were no middlemen, no contracts, no royalty cuts.

Asha had full control.

And the best part? She didn't even need a studio.

Her AI assistant helped her write the melody, arrange the beats, and master the final track.

Welcome to the AI + Blockchain Creator Economy — a world where artists are free, global, and in full control of their work.

THE RISE OF AI-GENERATED NFTS

Once upon a time, if you were a musician, a painter, a poet, or even a filmmaker — you needed someone to "give you a chance." Maybe a record label, an art gallery, a production house. They controlled your path, and often, your earnings.

Not anymore.

With AI and blockchain, that power has shifted.

Artists are now using AI tools like DALL·E, Midjourney, Aiva, and MuseNet to generate high-quality digital art and music — quickly, affordably, and uniquely. These creations are then minted as NFTs (non-fungible tokens) on blockchain platforms.

What does this mean?

It means:

- The art or music becomes a digital asset with proof of ownership.
- It can be bought, sold, or traded, just like a painting or vinyl record.
- And the artist gets paid instantly whenever it's purchased or resold.

A 16-year-old in Jaipur can now paint with pixels using AI and sell her work to collectors in London. A college band in Pune can upload their songs as music NFTs and earn from every single download—without losing a single rupee to middlemen.

WHAT MAKES IT REVOLUTIONARY?

AI empowers the creator

Even if you don't know how to code music or sketch with a brush, AI can help. You feed it your idea—say, "a classical Indian melody mixed with futuristic synth"—and it helps you build a masterpiece.

Blockchain secures the creation

Once your song or artwork is turned into an NFT, it's yours forever. It can't be copied without record. It can't be stolen or forged. Every transaction is public, traceable, and permanent.

The fans are the sponsors

No longer do you need millions of followers. A small, loyal community can directly support you by buying your music, art, or limited-edition NFTs. You keep almost everything you earn.

THE REAL-WORLD MAGIC: ASHA'S STORY

Let's return to Asha from Kolkata.

She used to perform in cafés and hope someone would notice her. Then one day, she heard about an AI music tool that could help her create full tracks.

With a little learning, she began writing and producing songs at home. Her friend helped her mint the tracks as NFTs on a decentralized platform like Audius or Royal.

Within months, she had fans in Europe and the U.S., who bought her music not just as listeners but as collectors. Some even resold her NFTs, and every time that happened, she received a royalty automatically, thanks to smart contracts.

No waiting. No chasing payments. No sharing profits with platforms.

THE RISE OF MUSIC & ART INDUSTRY

This isn't just about one artist. This is about a new kind of economy — the Creator Economy 2.0 — where AI and blockchain create new rules.

▶ MUSIC PLATFORMS GO DECENTRALIZED

Web3 music sites are cutting out streaming giants. Artists upload directly, set their price, and control how royalties work. No more "0.003 rupees per stream."

▶ ART EXHIBITIONS GO VIRTUAL

Artists host NFT exhibitions in the Metaverse. You walk through digital galleries, see AI-made art, and buy the pieces you love in Ethereum or MATIC.

▶ COLLABORATIONS GO GLOBAL

A beat producer in Delhi can collaborate with a singer in Ghana — both using AI tools — and release a hit together as an NFT. The system tracks their shares and pays each of them automatically.

WHY IT MATTERS FOR INDIA

India is already a land full of talent. But for decades, that talent was locked behind barriers:

- Language
- Gatekeepers
- Money
- Location

But with AI and blockchain, all of that is disappearing.

You don't need to be in Mumbai to make it big in music. You don't need to live in Paris to sell your paintings. You don't need to wait for someone to sign you.

You just need an idea, a device, and the will to learn.

The AI + Blockchain Creator Economy isn't a replacement for human creativity — it's a partner.

It gives everyday artists tools, ownership, and income.

For the first time, your digital painting can be as valuable as a real one. Your AI-assisted song can tour the world without you leaving your bedroom.

In this new world, creativity is currency — and you hold the power.

Asha's rooftop in Kolkata is now a global stage.

And tomorrow, it could be yours.

AI & BLOCKCHAIN IN THE JOB MARKET – A WORLD WITHOUT HR?

Bangalore, 2035,

The monsoon rain tapped softly on the window as Aryan adjusted his VR headset and entered his digital workspace. A few years ago, Aryan was just a struggling freelance designer trying to find clients online, constantly chasing payments, emailing resumes, and competing with thousands of others.

Today, his workday began with a soft chime — an AI notification.

"You've been matched with a Metaverse development project. Deadline: 5 days. Payment: 1,200 USDT in escrow. Shall I accept?"

Aryan smiled. No interviews. No long chats with HR. Just skill, verified reputation, and blockchain-backed trust. He nodded, and the system instantly accepted the project. The smart contract had already locked the payment in a secure crypto wallet. As soon as he submitted the final build of the virtual museum — a beautifully designed interactive experience — the funds would automatically be released. No need to chase anyone. No awkward invoice reminders.

A NEW WAY TO WORK

The job market has seen many revolutions: industrial, digital, remote. But what we're witnessing now is something deeper. With the combination of Artificial Intelligence (AI) and Blockchain, we're entering an age where trust, skill, and speed are all built into the system.

Here's how it works:

SKILL OVER DEGREES

Traditional hiring often relied on resumes, interviews, and background checks — a long process filled with bias, delays, and paperwork. But now, AI systems scan blockchain-verified credentials. These aren't just paper degrees; they're time-stamped, tamper-proof records of skills, projects, ratings, and feedback. So, whether you learned UX design from a YouTube course or coding from a blockchain bootcamp, the system recognizes your actual work — not just your qualifications.

INSTANT HIRING, NO MIDDLEMEN

Platforms powered by AI use advanced algorithms to match talent with projects in real-time. You don't have to apply to dozens of job boards. If your blockchain profile shows you're skilled in 3D modeling, you might wake up tomorrow with a project offer from a company in Tokyo or Toronto.

SMART CONTRACTS REPLACE HR

Once hired, the payment process is handled by smart contracts. These are self-executing pieces of code on the blockchain that hold the payment, monitor deadlines, and release the money when the task is completed. No managers, no payroll systems, no delays.

Aryan's experience wasn't unique.

In fact, in 2035, over 30% of digital freelancers worldwide work via decentralized job platforms that use AI to match skills and blockchain to handle contracts and payments. It's fast, efficient, and global.

Another major benefit of this new system is fairness. AI systems — when properly designed — don't discriminate based on gender, race, geography, or appearance. They assess skills, experience, and past ratings. Blockchain ensures the records can't be faked or manipulated.

A young designer from Imphal gets the same opportunity as someone from Mumbai. A coder in a remote Uttarakhand town gets hired by a company in New York — without ever leaving their home. And since payments are made in crypto, no one waits weeks for international transfers.

It's a world without borders, without resumes, and without red tape.

A WORLD WITHOUT HR?

That's the big question. Will this new system replace HR departments entirely?

Not completely. Human roles will always matter — for leadership, for empathy, for creative collaboration. But many repetitive tasks — like resume screening, payroll processing, contract drafting — are now handled by AI and smart contracts.

Imagine a small startup of just five people hiring talent across the globe, managing payments, verifying work histories — all without an HR department. That's no longer science fiction. That's daily reality in the Web3 job world.

THE RISE OF THE DIGITAL RESUME

In this new world, your "resume" isn't a PDF. It's a living blockchain identity.

Every project you complete, every client review, every payment — it's all part of your decentralized work history. No one can fake it. No one can delete it. And it's accessible anywhere in the world.

For freelancers, this means freedom. For companies, it means faster, fairer, and smarter hiring.

As Aryan submitted the final design files and received his payment in crypto within minutes, he leaned back in his chair. No stress. No delay. Just honest work and honest reward.

The job market hadn't disappeared — it had simply evolved.

And in this new world, your skill is your passport, your blockchain ID is your reputation, and AI is your personal hiring manager.

The future of work is already here.

And it's smarter, fairer, and more exciting than we ever imagined.

THE RISE OF AI-POWERED DAOS – COMPANIES WITHOUT CEOS?

Mumbai, 2035,

The sun was just rising over the Arabian Sea when Ayaan walked into his apartment. It wasn't just any weekday. He had just received a notification that made him pause with surprise and pride.

"Your proposal for the new product feature has been approved by 78% of token holders. Implementation begins Monday."

Ayaan wasn't working in a regular startup anymore. There was no CEO, no manager to report to, and no endless Zoom meetings filled with corporate jargon. He was a part of something different — a new kind of company. A *DAO*.

And this one was run not by people in corner offices, but by AI algorithms and blockchain-based smart contracts.

WHAT EXACTLY IS A DAO?

Let's rewind a little.

A DAO stands for Decentralized Autonomous Organization. Think of it like a digital company — but with no traditional hierarchy, no central boss, and no office politics.

Instead of being controlled by a CEO or a management team, a DAO is governed by code — transparent, programmable logic stored on the blockchain.

Here's how it works:

- **Smart contracts** (self-running computer programs) define how the organization operates.
- **AI** can help in making intelligent decisions — from analyzing project proposals to suggesting salaries.
- **Token holders** (employees, investors, or users) vote on key matters like product updates, budget allocation, or partnerships.

In short, everyone has a voice, and every decision is recorded — openly, securely, and without bias.

A STARTUP WITHOUT A CEO

Let's picture a real scenario in 2035:

It's the year 2035. In the bustling lanes of Mumbai's Powai, a group of passionate young engineers, designers, and educators gather in a cozy co-working space. Their mission? To create a powerful AI-based learning app that brings quality education to rural kids across India. But they're not thinking about getting an office, raising VC funds, or registering a private company.

They're building something new—a DAO, or Decentralized Autonomous Organization.

Now, what's that?

A DAO isn't like a traditional company with a CEO, HR manager, or board of directors. Instead, it's a digital community that runs on rules coded into a blockchain. No paperwork, no middlemen. Just pure collaboration and shared ownership. It's like if WhatsApp groups had governance, salaries, budgets, and a transparent treasury—automated by smart contracts and open to everyone who contributes.

In this DAO, everything is defined through smart contracts—digital agreements that no one can tamper with. From how salaries are paid to how decisions are made; the system runs itself. AI also plays a role, monitoring contributions and adjusting payments based on real performance and feedback.

There are no long HR rounds or weekly board meetings. Proposals are made by members, discussed openly, voted on by the community, and if approved—executed instantly. The funds are stored in a blockchain wallet, where every transaction is visible and auditable in real time. No hidden costs, no shady dealings—just crystal-clear transparency.

Meet Ayaan, a 26-year-old developer from Thane. He's not employed by this startup. In fact, he's never even met the core team in person. But he's a member of the DAO. He connects his crypto wallet, browses the open tasks, picks what he loves—coding a new

AI feature—and submits his work. The community reviews it, votes, and if approved, he gets paid in crypto instantly.

No interview. No notice period. Just skill, trust, and freedom.

People from all corners of India are contributing. A designer from Hyderabad, a teacher from Himachal, a voice artist from Assam. They all bring in their skills, earn fairly, and help shape the project's direction. This isn't freelancing. It's not employment. It's ownership without paperwork, powered by technology and community.

And the best part? The platform they're building is helping students in rural Bihar, Jharkhand, and Odisha get AI-powered personalized lessons—even where there's no regular school teacher.

This is what the future of work looks like.

Decentralized. Fair. Transparent. And inclusive.

No more gatekeeping. No more bureaucracy. Just humans and machines working together, openly and globally.

In a world where AI brings intelligence and blockchain brings trust, DAOs are giving rise to a new kind of entrepreneurship—one where you don't need to be rich, famous, or well-connected to build something impactful. All you need is your skill, your voice, and your wallet.

The revolution isn't coming. It's already here. And it's open to anyone with Wi-Fi and a dream.

HOW AI MAKES IT ALL POSSIBLE

While blockchain provides transparency and security, AI brings the brainpower.

- AI systems scan all incoming project proposals and filter the best ones.

- AI analyzes past budgets and market trends to suggest smart financial plans.
- It even writes the first draft of smart contracts, which are then reviewed by the DAO community.

Over time, the AI learns — improving decisions, automating routine tasks, and flagging risks. With every vote and every interaction, it becomes smarter.

In many DAOs, the community no longer needs dozens of managers. AI handles most of the work.

But it doesn't mean people are replaced. It means people are freed — to create, innovate, and collaborate instead of just supervising.

THE BENEFITS OF AI-POWERED DAOS

This model of working offers massive advantages:

FAIRNESS

Since AI makes decisions based on logic and data, it reduces human bias. And because all rules are programmed into smart contracts, no one can secretly break them.

TRANSPARENCY

Every vote, every payout, every action is recorded on the blockchain. No hidden clauses. No shady backroom deals.

GLOBAL ACCESS

You don't need a visa or an office cubicle. If you have skills and internet, you can participate — whether you live in Delhi or a village in Odisha.

24/7 OPERATIONS

With AI and smart contracts, the organization never sleeps. Ideas are evaluated in real time. Decisions don't wait for boardroom meetings.

BUT IS THIS FUTURE SAFE?

Of course, every revolution has its risks. And the DAO model isn't perfect yet.

AI BIAS

If the AI is trained on flawed data, it can make unfair decisions. That's why diverse datasets and regular audits are crucial.

SECURITY THREATS

A bug in a smart contract can lead to big financial losses. Hackers can target DAO wallets or manipulate voting systems.

JOB DISPLACEMENT

Many traditional roles – like middle management, HR, or finance processing – might shrink or disappear entirely.

But as history shows, every tech wave kills some jobs and creates new ones. In the DAO world, we'll see a rise in roles like:

- Smart Contract Auditors
- AI Behavior Trainers
- Governance Designers
- Community Architects

Instead of fighting the change, people are learning to work *with* it.

How to Prepare for This Future

"Future-Ready Checklist"

- ✓ Learn how smart contracts work
- ✓ Start using DeFi platforms with AI analytics
- ✓ Explore AI-powered tools like ChatGPT, MidJourney, or DALL·E
- ✓ Understand DAOs and decentralized identity (DID)
- ✓ Keep up with regulations in your country
- ✓ Consider learning Solidity (for smart contract development) or Python (for AI)

A MORE DEMOCRATIC FUTURE?

DAOs aren't just changing how we work. They're reshaping how power is distributed.

In the traditional world, power sits at the top. A few decide for many. But in DAOs, **everyone with a token has a say**. It's like a digital democracy, where votes are not just about elections – they're about features, budgets, and community vision.

For young Indians who've grown up with smartphones, crypto wallets, and global exposure, this feels natural. They no longer dream of climbing a corporate ladder. They dream of *building* ladders – open ones, where others can climb too.

Not the End, But a New Beginning...

Ayaan's phone buzzed again. Payment received — 1,200 USDT for his last completed sprint. He smiled. No invoices. No follow-ups. No office politics.

The project continues to grow. The DAO is now planning a global partnership with educators in Brazil and Nigeria. And every contributor — from coders to content creators — will get a share of the profits.

This isn't just a job.

It's ownership. It's freedom. It's the future.

The rise of AI-powered DAOs isn't about removing humans. It's about giving them more power — to choose, to create, and to lead.

We may not need CEOs anymore.

Because now, we have something better.

A community. A code. And a vision shared by all.

In the next decade, those who control data and those who protect it will not be the same. The future belongs to those who can do both—with intelligence and integrity.

******

"The great enemy of freedom is concentration of power. Blockchain is the antidote."

©Milton Friedman (Economist, Nobel Laureate)

CHAPTER SEVEN

THE BATTLE FOR DIGITAL FREEDOM – GOVERNMENTS VS. DECENTRALIZATION

> *"You can't stop things like Bitcoin. It will be everywhere and the world will have to readjust. Governments can't stop it."*
>
> – *John McAfee, Cybersecurity Pioneer*

New Delhi, 2035,

A group of policymakers sit inside the RBI headquarters, staring at real-time financial data projected on holographic screens.

The numbers are shocking.

✓ 70% of Indian businesses now settle international transactions using Bitcoin or stablecoins, bypassing the banking system.

- ✓ Millions of young Indians work for decentralized autonomous organizations (DAOs), earning in Ethereum, Solana, and Digital Rupees.
- ✓ Traditional tax collection methods are failing, as people use privacy-focused DeFi protocols to manage wealth.

Across the street, in a bustling cybercafé, 24-year-old Anika sits with her laptop, scrolling through her earnings. She's a Metaverse architect, designing virtual cities for a DAO based in Dubai.

Her income? Paid in Bitcoin.

Her savings? Locked in a decentralized wallet.

Her taxes? Difficult for the government to track.

This is the new financial reality—a world where people no longer need banks or governments to control their money.

Some call it freedom.
Governments call it chaos.

And now, the world is witnessing the biggest power struggle of the digital age:

Governments vs. Decentralization.

THE RISE OF DIGITAL FREEDOM – A WORLD WITHOUT BORDERS

For most of human history, the power to create and control money rested in the hands of rulers, governments, and financial institutions.

In ancient kingdoms, coins were minted under the authority of the crown, stamped with the ruler's image as a symbol of legitimacy. The state's control over gold reserves dictated the economic life of its citizens. In modern times, banks inherited this role. They regulated the flow of credit, determined interest rates, and decided who could access capital. The rise of credit card companies further concentrated financial authority, enabling corporations to dictate lending terms and define creditworthiness.

For the individual, participation in the economy required compliance. Trust in these centralized institutions was not optional — it was the price of entry into modern life.

Then came the blockchain revolution.

At its core, blockchain removed the need for institutional trust. Cryptocurrencies like Bitcoin operated on decentralized networks, verified not by governments or banks, but by distributed consensus. Decentralized finance (DeFi) extended this principle, offering lending, borrowing, and trading without intermediaries. In parallel, the emerging Metaverse economy introduced entirely digital marketplaces, where land, labor, and value could be exchanged beyond geographical or political boundaries.

For the first time, individuals could store value without a bank, transact without a state-issued currency, and engage in financial systems without centralized oversight. Money became purely digital. Finance became inherently borderless. Trust shifted from human institutions to immutable code.

From a governmental perspective, this transformation was not merely technological — it was existential. The ability to control the monetary system has historically been one of the strongest levers of state power. It enables taxation, regulation, and economic influence. When blockchain technology bypasses these levers, it disrupts centuries of economic governance.

The challenge now is twofold. For citizens, it is about understanding and responsibly participating in this new landscape. For governments, it is about adapting to a world where monetary authority is no longer a given, and where decentralization challenges traditional models of economic control.

The battle for digital freedom is not an abstract debate — it is an unfolding reality, reshaping the balance between state, market, and individual. The question is no longer whether decentralization will change the financial order, but how — and at what cost — this transition will redefine power in the 21st century.

> *"Bitcoin isn't just money for the internet — it's a separation of money and state."*
>
> *----Andreas M. Antonopoulos*

WHY GOVERNMENTS FEAR DECENTRALIZATION

Decentralized finance (DeFi), cryptocurrencies, and blockchain technology remove middlemen and give financial power directly to individuals.

These creates a major problem for governments:

LOST CONTROL OVER MONEY SUPPLY

- Governments print money to manage economies.
- Cryptocurrencies, with fixed supplies, can't be manipulated.
- If people stop using fiat, governments lose their ability to control inflation.

DIFFICULT TO TAX CRYPTO TRANSACTIONS

- People earn in Bitcoin or stablecoins, often outside government oversight.
- Decentralized exchanges (DEXs) allow peer-to-peer trading with no reporting.

- Taxation becomes nearly impossible.

WEAKENING OF CENTRALIZED FINANCIAL INSTITUTIONS

- Banks lose customers as people store wealth in decentralized wallets.
- Stock markets decline as companies issue tokenized assets instead of shares.
- National currencies lose value as global trade moves to crypto.

RISE OF PRIVACY & UNTRACEABLE TRANSACTIONS

- Privacy coins (Monero, Zcash) make it impossible to track transactions.
- People use blockchain-based identities instead of government-issued IDs.

For the first time in history, individuals have more financial freedom than governments.

And governments are fighting back.

THE GLOBAL WAR ON CRYPTO – REGULATIONS VS. RESISTANCE

As crypto adoption skyrocketed, governments worldwide responded in different ways:

CHINA – THE CRYPTO BAN STRATEGY

- ✓ 2017: China bans ICOs (Initial Coin Offerings).

- ✓ 2021: China bans Bitcoin mining, calling it "a threat to financial stability."
- ✓ 2022-2025: The government introduces Digital Yuan (CBDC) as an alternative.

RESULT?

- ✓ Bitcoin mining shifted to other countries.
- ✓ Crypto activity went underground.
- ✓ China's Digital Yuan gained adoption—but didn't stop DeFi growth.

USA – THE REGULATION APPROACH

- ✓ 2023-2026: The U.S. launches strict crypto tax laws.
- ✓ 2027: The government introduces Federal Stablecoins, pegged to the U.S. dollar.
- ✓ 2030: Big tech firms launch their own digital currencies (AmazonCoin, ApplePay Token).

Result?

- ✓ Institutional investors adopt Bitcoin.
- ✓ Crypto-backed mortgages & loans become mainstream.
- ✓ People still use decentralized wallets to bypass surveillance.

INDIA – THE BALANCING ACT

- ✓ 2022: India imposes 30% tax on crypto gains.

- ✓ 2024: RBI launches Digital Rupee (CBDC) for national transactions.
- ✓ 2028: Government integrates blockchain for public services while limiting privacy coins.

RESULT?

- ✓ Digital Rupee gains massive adoption.
- ✓ Crypto taxation increases but doesn't stop adoption.
- ✓ DeFi continues growing through global platforms.

Governments are realizing they can't ban crypto.

So instead, they're trying to control it.

THE FUTURE OF DIGITAL FREEDOM – WHO WINS?

The battle between governments and decentralization isn't just about finance.

It's about control vs. freedom.

Governments want:

- ❖ To regulate every financial transaction.
- ❖ To maintain centralized control over money.
- ❖ To keep taxation and compliance mandatory.

People want:

- ❖ Financial independence from banks.
- ❖ Privacy & borderless transactions.

- ❖ Freedom to store wealth in decentralized assets.

THREE POSSIBLE SCENARIOS FOR THE FUTURE

Scenario 1: Governments Fully Adopt Crypto & Blockchain

CBDCs (Central Bank Digital Currencies) replace cash.
Crypto transactions become regulated, but not banned.
Hybrid financial systems emerge (traditional + decentralized finance).

Scenario 2: Governments Fight Crypto, But Lose Control

Privacy coins & decentralized platforms thrive.
People move wealth into unstoppable DeFi ecosystems.
Crypto adoption spreads, weakening national currencies.

Scenario 3: Total Government Control Over Digital Finance

CBDCs fully replace cash, with surveillance over every transaction.
Crypto use becomes highly restricted or illegal.
Financial freedom is lost, and people are forced into centralized systems.
The question isn't just who wins.

The question is: Will individuals fight for digital freedom, or accept government control?

2035: A DAY IN THE FUTURE OF FINANCE

- ✓ 8:00 AM – Ankita pays for groceries using Digital Rupees, but her privacy settings automatically convert some funds into Bitcoin.
- ✓ 12:00 PM – Her salary is paid in Ethereum by a global DAO, with smart contracts handling taxation.

- ✓ 3:00 PM – She takes out a crypto-backed loan to buy property in a decentralized smart city.
- ✓ 6:00 PM – The government introduces new DeFi restrictions, but people find alternatives through decentralized exchanges.

The world isn't fully decentralized yet.

But governments are no longer the only power in finance.

The fight for digital freedom has just begun.

Questions to Remember

- **The issue is not who wins** – governments or crypto.
- **The issue is:** Will individuals fight for digital freedom or surrender it for convenience?

******

"The cities of the future will run on intelligence–both artificial and human–powered by technology that puts people, not governments, at the center."

©Elon Musk

CHAPTER EIGHT

THE SMART CITIES OF THE FUTURE – BLOCKCHAIN-POWERED NATIONS

"Smart cities need smart trust. Blockchain brings that trust by making systems open, verifiable, and citizen-driven."

- Vitalik Buterin (Creator of Ethereum)

Mumbai, 2040,

The streets of Mumbai don't look the same anymore.

Gone are the chaotic traffic jams, long lines at banks, and endless bureaucracy. The city has transformed into a hyper-connected, AI-driven, blockchain-powered metropolis.

Streetlights adjust in real time based on pedestrian movement. Autonomous electric taxis operate without human drivers. Solar-powered buildings trade excess energy with each other via blockchain smart contracts—no government oversight required.

At Chhatrapati Shivaji Maharaj International Airport, Aarav walks past facial-recognition security gates. His digital ID, stored on a blockchain, eliminates the need for immigration officers.

In the heart of the city, a towering Metaverse business hub operates entirely in virtual reality—where Indian entrepreneurs collaborate with teams from across the world without stepping outside their homes.

Mumbai, like many cities, has become part of a new global phenomenon:

Blockchain-Powered Smart Cities.

These are not just technologically advanced urban centres.

These are self-sustaining, decentralized digital nations, run by code, AI, and smart contracts, rather than governments and bureaucracy.

And this is only the beginning.

WHAT ARE SMART CITIES?

A Smart City is an urban area that uses technology, AI, and blockchain to make infrastructure more efficient, sustainable, and decentralized.

Traditional cities rely on:

- Government-run systems (banks, energy, healthcare).
- Bureaucratic processes (permits, taxes, legal contracts).
- Middlemen (brokers, real estate agents, banks).

But Smart Cities operate autonomously, using blockchain-based governance, AI-driven automation, and digital financial systems.

Think of them as real-world versions of DAOs (Decentralized Autonomous Organizations), where the city itself is run by smart contracts and AI.

Future Nation = Transparency (Blockchain) + Intelligence (AI) + Connectivity (IoT)

HOW BLOCKCHAIN IS POWERING SMART CITIES

Smart cities are more than just Wi-Fi zones and digital payments. They are about creating trust, transparency, and efficiency in how a city functions. This is where blockchain comes in. Imagine a city where land records can't be forged, electricity bills are automatically settled, and traffic systems run on real-time, tamper-proof data. Blockchain ensures every transaction — whether financial, legal, or civic — is stored securely and openly, removing corruption and delays.

From Bengaluru experimenting with blockchain-based property records, to Dubai's vision of becoming the first blockchain-powered government, cities worldwide are realizing that decentralization is the backbone of smart governance. For citizens, this means faster services, reduced red tape, and more control over their own data. For governments, it means efficiency, accountability, and better resource management.

In short, blockchain is not just powering smart cities — it is making them trustworthy, citizen-driven, and future-ready.

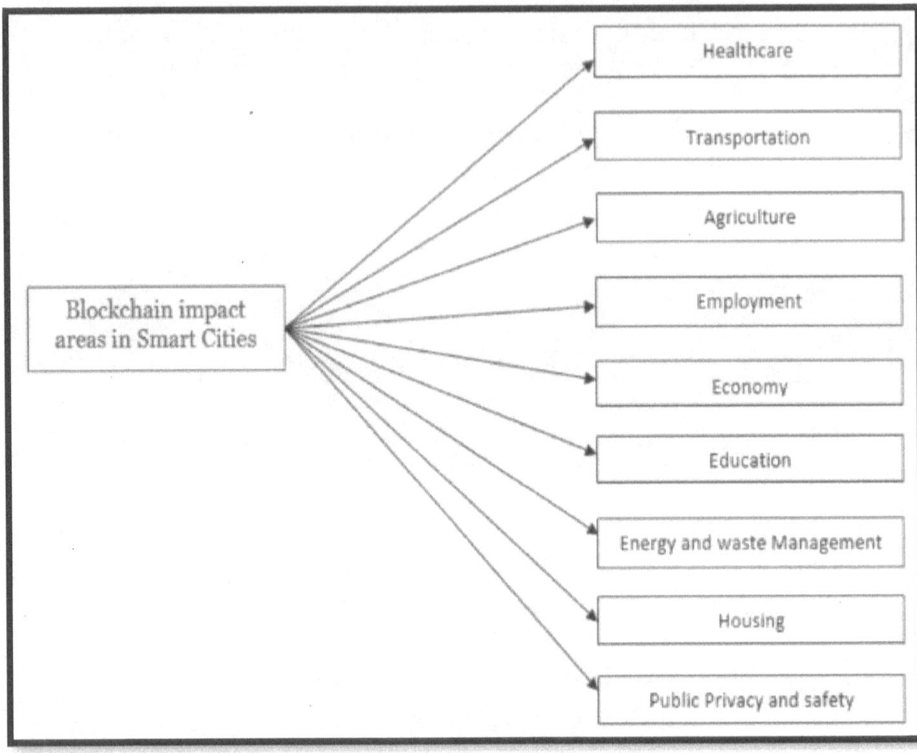

DIGITAL IDENTITY & GOVERNANCE

PROBLEM: Governments control citizens' identities, voting rights, and access to services.

SOLUTION: Blockchain-based digital IDs give people full control over their personal data.

REAL-WORLD EXAMPLE

AADHAAR 2.0 (India's decentralized identity system)

Mumbai, 2040,

Sunita stood in line at a small municipal office, not to fill out forms or submit documents, but just to scan her eye. Within seconds, her blockchain-based digital ID confirmed her identity, pulled up her records, and issued her land registration certificate. No paperwork. No middlemen. No bribes.

This wasn't just a new system. It was a new relationship between citizens and the government.

For decades, governments around the world held absolute control over identity systems. From passports to voter cards, every piece of personal data passed through layers of bureaucracy, vulnerable to tampering, theft, and inefficiency. But with the evolution of blockchain, a new kind of digital ID emerged — one that gave power back to the people.

Enter Aadhaar 2.0 — India's decentralized digital identity revolution.

Built on a secure, public blockchain, Aadhaar 2.0 is more than just a number. It's a self-sovereign identity — meaning only the individual controls their data. From academic degrees to birth certificates, from medical records to financial statements, all information is encrypted, stored on-chain, and accessible only through user permission.

This means Sunita can now:

- Vote in elections while working remotely in Singapore.
- Access government subsidies in real-time without filling out forms.
- Apply for jobs, take online courses, or renew licenses — all without stepping foot in an office.

More importantly, she doesn't need to trust a centralized database or worry about data leaks. Everything is protected by cryptography, time-stamped on the blockchain, and verifiable without disclosing unnecessary information.

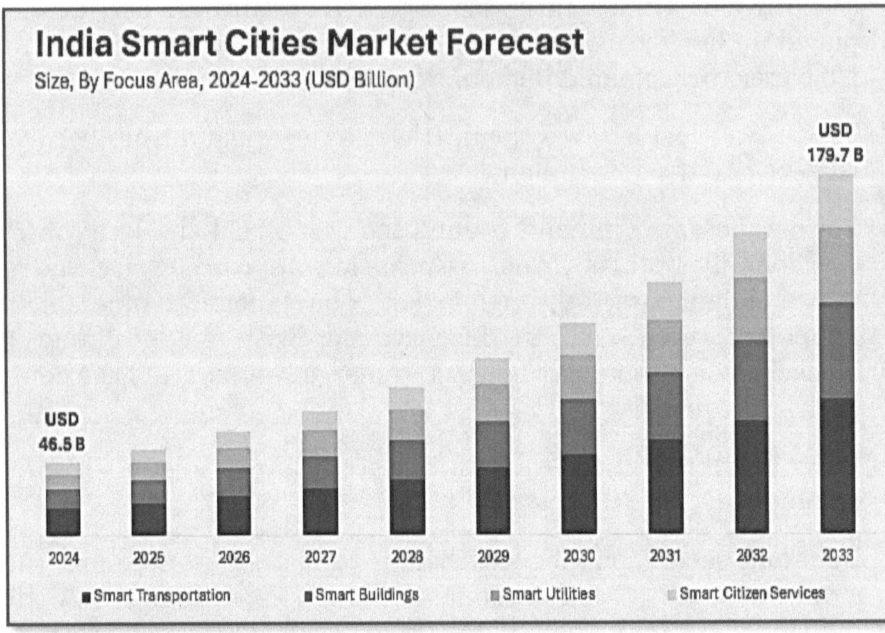

WHY DOES THIS MATTER?

In a world moving toward full digitization, the foundation of all services — banking, healthcare, education — starts with identity. Without a secure, universally accepted, and user-controlled identity system, access becomes fragmented and unfair.

Traditional systems struggle with duplication, fraud, and exclusion. Aadhaar 2.0 solves these by using zero-knowledge proofs — a type of blockchain cryptography that lets someone prove their identity without revealing the actual data.

REAL-WORLD INSPIRATION: ESTONIA'S E-RESIDENCY & INDIA'S AADHAAR

Estonia was one of the first countries to pioneer digital governance. Citizens and even foreigners can become "e-residents," start businesses, file taxes, and access government services online. India, with Aadhaar 1.0, built the largest biometric ID system in the world.

Now, with Aadhaar 2.0 moving to the blockchain, India is combining its digital scale with cutting-edge decentralization.

Imagine voting in the 2044 general elections — from your living room in Dubai — using a blockchain-secured Aadhaar ID.

That's not science fiction. That's the promise of digital freedom.

SMART INFRASTRUCTURE – ENERGY, TRANSPORT, AND UTILITIES

PROBLEM: Cities waste massive resources due to inefficient systems.

SOLUTION: Blockchain automates energy grids, public transport, and resource management.

Delhi, 2040,

As dusk settles over the city, Delhi doesn't turn its lights on all at once.

Instead, the streetlights flicker to life one by one, reacting to real-time pedestrian data. A delivery drone zips quietly through the air, guided by AI traffic sensors that predict wind flow. Down below, electric buses reroute themselves based on live demand, all without human intervention.

There's no control room, no frantic dispatchers — just code.

This is the new face of urban life: smart infrastructure, built not by bureaucrats but by AI and blockchain working together in harmony.

THE PROBLEM WITH TRADITIONAL INFRASTRUCTURE

For decades, cities have relied on centralized institutions to manage roads, electricity, water, waste, and transport. While effective in many ways, these systems often fail due to inefficiencies, corruption, human error, and lack of real-time adaptability.

Energy gets wasted. Traffic piles up. Resources are mismanaged. And services don't reach those who need them most.

Now imagine a city where:

- Buildings generate solar power and sell the surplus automatically.
- Water pipes detect and repair leaks before anyone notices.
- Public transport dynamically adjusts routes based on real-time user needs.

This isn't fantasy.

Its smart infrastructure powered by blockchain.

HOW IT WORKS

Smart infrastructure uses a combination of AI (to analyze, predict, and automate actions) and blockchain (to securely log and verify those actions without bias or tampering).

Let's break it down:

ENERGY GRIDS

Buildings equipped with solar panels automatically sell excess power to nearby homes or industries. Every unit of energy is tokenized and recorded on the blockchain — no power cuts, no bills, no middlemen.

TRANSPORT SYSTEMS

AI-powered public transit reads rider demand in real time. Buses, metros, and taxis reroute themselves using decentralized logistics platforms. Passengers pay in crypto or via their digital wallet — and every payment is recorded immutably.

WASTE & WATER MANAGEMENT

IoT sensors report issues to decentralized networks. Smart contracts automatically schedule maintenance, triggering payments when tasks are completed. No bribes, no delays.

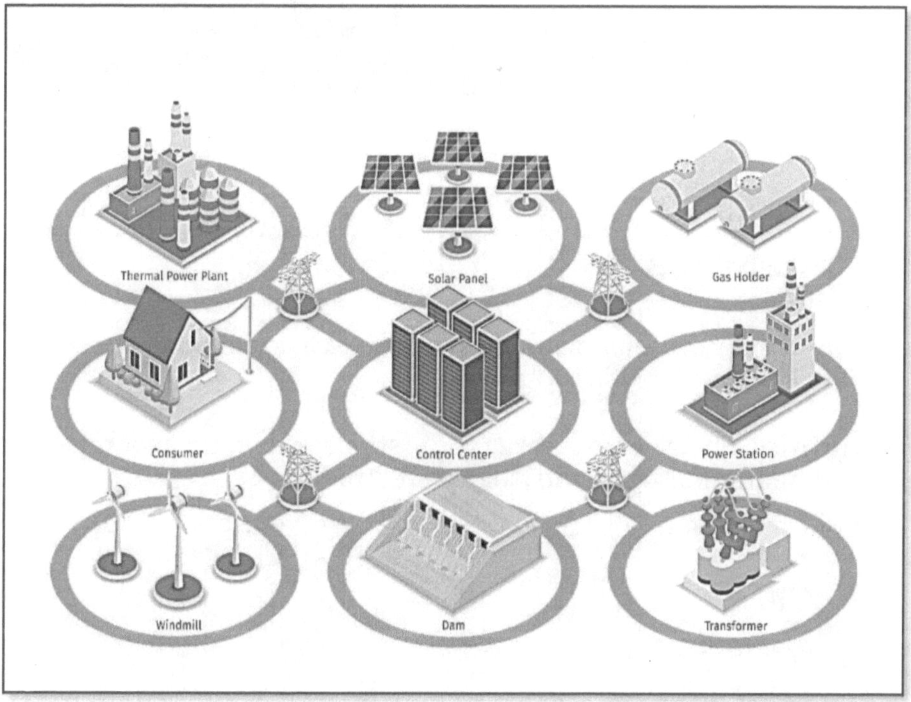

Figure: Smart Infrastructure - Energy, Transport, and Utilities

REAL-WORLD EXAMPLE: DUBAI'S SMART CITY INITIATIVE

Dubai has become one of the global leaders in integrating blockchain into city services. As early as the 2020s, Dubai aimed to move 100% of all government transactions — from property sales to business permits — onto a blockchain.

Now, in 2040, that vision has matured.

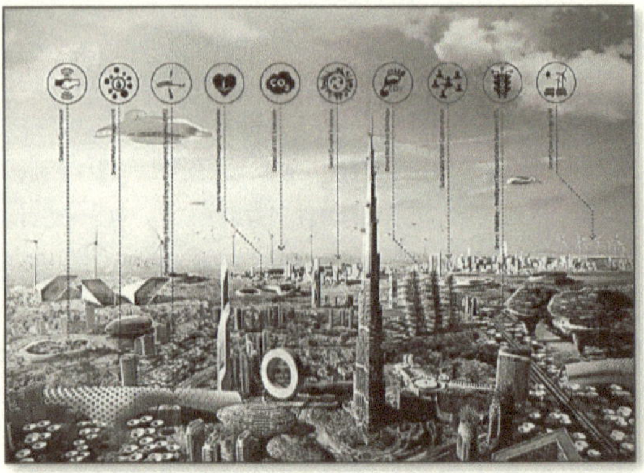

Citizens use digital IDs to access public services. Property is traded entirely via smart contracts. Electricity flows peer-to-peer. And every ride on the metro is logged in a transparent, tamper-proof system that no one can manipulate — not even the government.

DECENTRALIZED FINANCE (DEFI) & DIGITAL CURRENCIES

Problem: Traditional banking systems exclude millions of people and rely on outdated infrastructure.

Solution: Smart cities use crypto, stablecoins, and blockchain-based finance for payments, loans, and trade.

Patna, 2040,

It's a warm morning in Patna's old market. Vendors roll up their shutters, kids rush to school with smart tablets, and Anmol, a 42-year-old vegetable seller, is already receiving payments on his wristband.

No cash.
No card swipes.
Just a quiet vibration and a digital chime.

He just received 120 Digital Rupees from a customer's crypto wallet. The money is already split automatically: 80% goes into his spending wallet, 20% into a savings vault powered by a DeFi platform that earns him daily interest.

No bank manager needed.
No paperwork.
No waiting in line.

This is not just fintech. This is financial freedom — powered by blockchain.

THE PROBLEM: BANKS NEVER REACHED EVERYONE

In a country as vast and diverse as India, access to banking has always been unequal. Despite progress, millions still remain underserved — especially in rural areas.

- Long queues.
- Tedious verification processes.
- Hidden fees.
- Biased lending.
- Delays in payment transfers.

Traditional banks move slowly and often prioritize the wealthy. That's where DeFi — or Decentralized Finance — changes the game.

THE DEFI REVOLUTION

DeFi replaces the traditional banking system with smart contracts and crypto platforms that are:

- ✓ **Borderless** – You can send/receive money from anywhere.
- ✓ **Permissionless** – No bank account needed.
- ✓ **Transparent** – Every transaction is visible on the blockchain.
- ✓ **Fast** – Settlements happen in seconds.

- ✓ **Fair** – No middlemen. No bias.

From loans and insurance to savings and investing — DeFi offers full banking without the bank.

WHAT DOES IT LOOK LIKE IN REAL LIFE?

Let's paint a picture:

SALARIES IN DIGITAL RUPEES OR CRYPTO

A freelancer in Jaipur earns in USDC (a stablecoin). She converts part into Digital Rupees to pay bills, while the rest stays in crypto to grow in value or earn interest.

LOANS WITHOUT PAPERWORK

A farmer in Odisha needs money for new irrigation pipes. Instead of waiting weeks for a loan officer, he connects to a DeFi app. AI verifies his land documents on blockchain, and he receives funds instantly — all via a smart contract.

PAYMENTS AT EVERY CORNER

From chai stalls to grocery chains, crypto wallets have become as common as QR codes. Street vendors in Shillong, shopkeepers in Agra, and taxi drivers in Chennai all accept crypto.

REAL-WORLD INSPIRATION: EL SALVADOR'S BITCOIN CITY

While India has taken a cautious but progressive route, El Salvador paved the way by declaring Bitcoin as legal tender in 2021. By 2040, their Bitcoin City runs entirely on blockchain — schools, hospitals, electricity, and even taxes.

Now, many cities in Asia and Africa are adopting this template – and India is crafting its own version with unique cultural and economic blends.

THE IMPACT: FREEDOM, FAIRNESS, AND EMPOWERMENT

What makes DeFi powerful isn't just technology – it's what it represents:

- ✓ Financial inclusion for the unbanked.
- ✓ Faster global payments for India's remote gig workers.
- ✓ Better lending options for small business owners.
- ✓ Protection from inflation and devaluation.

With DeFi, control shifts from institutions to individuals. People no longer have to trust a system – they trust code.

By 2040, many cities worldwide operate on crypto-based economies.

REAL ESTATE & LAND OWNERSHIP ON BLOCKCHAIN

Problem: Buying property involves brokers, delays, corruption, and fraud.

Solution: Blockchain replaces property deeds with digital ownership records.

Lucknow, 2040,

The early morning sunlight poured through the windows as Ravi and Meera sat with their cups of chai. But their minds weren't on breakfast.

Today was the day.

After months of searching, saving, and planning, they were finally ready to buy their first apartment – a beautiful 2BHK on the 7th floor of a newly developed residential complex in Gomti Nagar.

But unlike their parents' generation, they weren't meeting brokers, waiting in lines at the registrar office, or collecting piles of legal documents.

Instead, they opened their laptops.

Ravi logged into a government-verified blockchain real estate portal. The listing for the apartment they wanted showed every detail – building approvals, title history, and even past transaction records, all stored immutably on the blockchain. There were no doubts, no grey areas.

With one click, a smart contract was generated. This digital agreement had all the necessary terms pre-programmed: the price, ownership transfer, payment method, and registration details.

Meera connected her Digital Rupee wallet, and they confirmed the payment.

Within seconds, the contract executed.
The funds were released.
The ownership was transferred.
And their new digital property deed arrived – safely stored in their wallet as a non-fungible token (NFT).

No agents.
No corruption.
No stress.

Just clean, fast, trustworthy property ownership.

WHY TRADITIONAL REAL ESTATE WAS A HEADACHE

Ask anyone in India who's ever tried to buy land or a flat, and you'll hear horror stories:

- **Paperwork confusion**: Multiple versions of land records, often handwritten or incomplete.
- **Fake sellers**: Land sold to multiple buyers at once, leading to court cases.
- **Endless delays**: Files "lost" in government offices. Months of back-and-forth.
- **Corruption**: Bribes demanded at every step.
- **Hidden costs**: Middlemen, stamp duty agents, shady brokers.

For most middle-class families, buying property was emotionally and financially exhausting.

HOW BLOCKCHAIN FIXES EVERYTHING

Blockchain technology brings something powerful to real estate: permanent, tamper-proof records that anyone can verify.

Let's break it down:

LAND TITLES AS NFTS

Each property is registered on the blockchain and represented by a unique NFT — a token that proves ownership. Just like you hold a share certificate, now you hold your land deed in a digital wallet.

SMART CONTRACTS REPLACE BROKERS & LAWYERS

Want to buy a flat? A smart contract can handle the agreement automatically — when the payment is made, the ownership transfers instantly.

FULL TRANSPARENCY

You can see the full history of a property: who owned it, for how long, for what price — all verified and visible.

NO PAPER, NO FRAUD

No more fake signatures, stolen documents, or illegal occupation. Once it's on the blockchain, it cannot be tampered with.

A REAL-LIFE GLIMPSE: DUBAI & SWEDEN

Dubai is already implementing blockchain for property registration. People can view listings, verify records, and complete deals from anywhere in the world – all online.

Sweden tested blockchain land registries too – and found it reduced property transaction time from 3 months to just a few hours.

Back home, states like Andhra Pradesh and Maharashtra are also working to bring land records on-chain – making India one of the leaders in this digital shift.

Imagine a farmer in Bihar wanting to lease a portion of his land to a solar company. With blockchain, he can verify ownership, sign a lease via a smart contract, and receive regular income – all digitally.

Or think of NRIs in Canada who want to buy property in India. No more risky relatives or shady agents. They can buy, verify, and register ownership right from their phone.

Even Metaverse-based property businesses are rising in cities like Pune and Bengaluru, helping people invest in both physical and digital real estate using blockchain.

Traditional City	**Blockchain-Powered Smart City**
Manual land records prone to fraud	Immutable blockchain-based land registry
High electricity theft	Smart contracts for energy usage & billing

Slow government services	Automated blockchain workflows
Citizen data stored in silos	Citizens own and control their identity
Paper-based contracts	Smart contracts execute instantly

AI-POWERED GOVERNANCE & CRIME PREVENTION

Problem: Government policies are often inefficient, slow, and corrupt.

Solution: AI + blockchain ensure transparent, data-driven governance.

Pune, 2040,

It's a Monday morning, but the city feels calm.

No honking, no angry traffic jams, no confusion at signals. Streets are moving smoothly. Waste trucks arrive exactly on time. Water tanks refill automatically. Even public parks report their own cleanliness status to the municipal dashboard.

This isn't a utopia — it's smart governance powered by AI and blockchain.

Sonal, a young civil servant, watches the city unfold on her transparent screen. She isn't buried in paperwork or files. Instead, she monitors real-time civic activity through a blockchain-integrated dashboard. Every part of the city — from electricity flow to law enforcement — runs like a well-oiled machine.

But how? The answer lies in self-executing code, AI prediction, and blockchain transparency.

WHAT IS SMART GOVERNANCE?

Traditionally, cities were managed with paperwork, endless approvals, and too much human involvement — which often led to delays, corruption, and inefficiency.

Smart governance changes that. It uses:

- AI to predict problems before they happen.
- **Blockchain** to automate and enforce laws without bias.
- **Smart contracts** to make city rules self-executing — no manual handling needed.

This means no more waiting in lines for approvals, no need to chase officers for updates, and no bribes under the table.

The city itself becomes intelligent — constantly learning, adapting, and enforcing its own rules.

HOW IT WORKS IN INDIA

India's urban planners and tech leaders have already begun testing these ideas.

Here's how it works step by step:

LAWS BECOME CODE

Imagine a law that says water bills must be paid by the 10th of every month. Instead of waiting for notices and reminders, a smart contract is written.

If you don't pay by the 10th, it automatically sends you a gentle nudge. Miss that too? A small late fee is added — all without human involvement.

And don't worry — these smart contracts can be updated democratically. Citizens vote digitally (via verified blockchain IDs), and changes are rolled out instantly.

CRIME PREVENTION GETS SMARTER

AI is trained to detect irregular patterns — like a sudden spike in electricity use (potential theft), or a sharp rise in water consumption at an unusual hour (pipe leakage or misuse).

It also scans financial transactions (stored anonymously on blockchain) to detect fraud, scams, or cyber threats.

Instead of chasing problems after they occur, cities predict and prevent them before they grow.

CITY SERVICES RUN AUTOMATICALLY

- ✓ Garbage bins alert the municipality when they're full.
- ✓ Streetlights turn on only when someone walks by.
- ✓ Public transport routes are adjusted daily based on live commuter data.

All this is possible because the city's entire operation is linked by blockchain, making it secure, trackable, and corruption-proof.

REAL-WORLD INSPIRATION: SINGAPORE'S AI-POWERED TRAFFIC SYSTEM

In Singapore, traffic fines are not given by cops chasing your car. Instead, AI-powered cameras monitor lanes and junctions. If you break a red light, the system detects it in real time, records the violation on blockchain, and issues a digital ticket.

There's no human argument, no missing files, and no bribe option.

And because everything is recorded permanently on the blockchain, you can always check your history, raise appeals transparently, or pay fines with a click.

This system is now inspiring cities like Bengaluru and Chennai to begin similar pilot programs.

WHY THIS MATTERS

Smart governance isn't just about flashy tech. It's about fairness, speed, and trust.

- **FOR THE GOVERNMENT:** More efficient systems, less corruption, better data.
- **FOR THE CITIZEN:** Faster services, more transparency, and greater control over how cities are run.

In 2040, no one should have to spend weeks chasing approvals to open a shop, install solar panels, or get a road repaired. With smart contracts and AI alerts, it all happens automatically — and you're always in the loop.

WILL SMART CITIES REPLACE NATIONS?

By 2040, many experts predict that smart cities will function like independent digital nations.

Some cities may:

- ✓ Issue their own digital currencies.
- ✓ Use AI-powered governance instead of elected officials.
- ✓ Attract global citizens who don't want to be tied to traditional governments.

Imagine a world where:

- ❖ A business owner in Mumbai operates under a decentralized city-state.
- ❖ A developer in Bangalore works remotely for a blockchain-powered city in Singapore.
- ❖ A retiree in Goa invests in a Metaverse-powered financial hub in Dubai.

National borders may no longer define where people live, work, or invest.

Instead, people may choose to be citizens of decentralized smart cities that align with their values and economic goals.

2035: A DAY IN A BLOCKCHAIN-POWERED SMART CITY

- ✓ 7:00 AM – Aarav wakes up in his solar-powered apartment, where energy bills are settled automatically via smart contracts.
- ✓ 10:00 AM – He attends a global business meeting in the Metaverse, collaborating with AI-driven teams across multiple cities.
- ✓ 2:00 PM – He buys property in Singapore's smart city district, using fractional real estate investment tokens.
- ✓ 5:00 PM – A smart contract automatically files his taxes, deducting payments in Digital Rupees and Ethereum.

- ✓ 8:00 PM – He enjoys an immersive VR Bollywood concert, with tickets stored as NFTs on the blockchain.

Aarav never visits a government office, never deals with banks, and never waits for approvals.

His city runs on code, automation, and decentralization.

And for the first time in history, he is in complete control of his wealth, work, and identity.

"In the future, streets will carry cars, but blockchains will carry trust."

******

"Crypto is not just money- it's a peaceful revolution against financial gatekeepers."

©Balaji Srinivasan (Former Coinbase CTO & Author of The Network State)

CHAPTER NINE

CRYPTO IN THE INDIAN ECONOMY – A SILENT REVOLUTION

First, they ignore you, then they laugh at you, then they fight you, then you win."

– *Mahatma Gandhi*

"You can ban an app. You can block a website. But can you stop an idea whose time has come?"

India is not just watching the crypto revolution happen — it is living it. Quietly, without much noise, millions of Indians have already become part of a financial system that's unlike anything we've seen before. It's fast, borderless, and most importantly — decentralized.

In this chapter, we'll explore how cryptocurrency is changing the Indian economy. We'll break it down in a friendly, simple way. Whether you're a complete beginner or someone who's curious about the real impact of crypto, this chapter is for you.

THE INDIAN FINANCIAL LANDSCAPE: A QUICK LOOK

India is a unique country when it comes to finance. On one hand, we have world-class digital payment systems like UPI (Unified Payments Interface) — which enables real-time money transfers 24/7. On the other, we still have large sections of the population who are unbanked or underbanked.

Despite technological progress, the average Indian still faces these challenges:

LIMITED ACCESS TO CREDIT

Traditional banks often require collateral, strong credit history, or formal employment proof. Most small shop owners, farmers, gig workers, or even salaried employees don't qualify.

SLOW CROSS-BORDER PAYMENTS

International remittances through SWIFT or bank wires can take several days and involve multiple intermediaries.

HIGH FEES ON MONEY TRANSFERS

Whether it's remitting money abroad or using wallets for domestic transactions, charges can eat into the value being transferred.

LOW FINANCIAL LITERACY

Many Indians struggle to understand financial products like insurance, mutual funds, or loans — let alone crypto.

Banks work, yes. But not for everyone. For many Indians, especially in small towns and villages, the financial system feels distant, slow, and expensive. This is where crypto steps in — offering a radically different and more inclusive alternative.

WHY CRYPTO MAKES SENSE FOR INDIA

India has three big strengths that make it perfect for crypto adoption.

DIGITAL SAVVY YOUTH

With over 600 million people under the age of 25, India is a youth-driven nation. This generation was born into mobile phones and internet culture. They are quick learners, fluent in digital apps, and naturally curious about emerging technologies. They are already using apps for banking, shopping, studying, and now — investing.

HIGH SMARTPHONE PENETRATION

Thanks to affordable Android phones and one of the world's cheapest internet data plans, smartphone usage has exploded — even in Tier 2, Tier 3 cities and villages. With a smartphone and an internet connection, anyone can download a crypto wallet and start transacting, no matter where they live.

GLOBAL WORKFORCE

India has a massive talent pool of freelancers — from software engineers to writers and marketers — working for clients across the world. Traditional payments like PayPal or wire transfers are slow and expensive. Crypto enables them to receive funds within minutes, with minimal fees, and sometimes even gain from appreciating currencies.

REAL-LIFE USE CASES

Let's look at how everyday Indians are using crypto in practical ways:

FREELANCERS AND REMOTE WORKERS

Meet Aakash, a 25-year-old graphic designer from Jaipur. He works with clients in the U.S. and Canada. Earlier, he had to wait 3–5 days to get paid via PayPal, and he'd lose 5–10% in conversion and transfer fees. Now? His clients send him stablecoins like USDT. He receives the funds in minutes — no bank needed, no middleman. He can then convert it into rupees via a crypto exchange, or hold on to it and watch it grow in value.

STUDENTS INVESTING SMALL AMOUNTS

Crypto platforms in India, such as CoinDCX and WazirX, let users start with as little as ₹100. Students like Priya from Chennai are investing in Bitcoin and Ethereum, not to become overnight millionaires, but to understand the world of digital finance. They're watching YouTube videos, joining Telegram communities, and learning about DeFi (decentralized finance) — a space once reserved for finance experts.

ARTISTS AND CREATORS

NFTs (non-fungible tokens) have opened new doors. Take Anjali, a digital illustrator in Delhi. She used to earn through client commissions. Now she mints her art on blockchain platforms and sells them as NFTs. Buyers from across the world pay her in ETH (Ethereum), and she retains full ownership and royalties for every resale — something unheard of in traditional art markets.

FAMILIES OF MIGRANT WORKERS

Lakhs of Indians work in the Gulf, Europe, and Southeast Asia, sending money back home. Traditional services like Western Union take up to 8% in fees and days to process. With crypto, a worker in Dubai can send USDT or Bitcoin to his family's wallet in Patna instantly — safely, and with negligible cost. Some platforms also allow conversion to rupees and direct deposit into bank accounts.

THE NUMBERS TELL THE STORY

- ✓ India ranks #1 in global crypto adoption according to Chainalysis, thanks to its massive retail usage.
- ✓ Over 20 million Indians are estimated to hold crypto — from metro cities to small towns.
- ✓ Indian investors collectively own over $200 billion worth of digital assets, growing year by year.
- ✓ India is home to 450+ blockchain startups, including global players like Polygon, which provides scalable Ethereum infrastructure and is valued in billions.

These are not just numbers. They are a sign that Indians are not just consumers of the crypto economy — they are becoming creators and innovators within it.

"Crypto in India is not just about profits; it's about participation – from chai stalls to tech parks, a silent revolution is building a borderless economy."

GOVERNMENT AND REGULATION: A COMPLICATED RELATIONSHIP

India's stance on crypto has been, to say the least, a rollercoaster.

A TIMELINE OF FLIP-FLOPS

- **2018**: RBI bans banks from dealing with crypto exchanges, citing financial instability.
- **2020**: Supreme Court lifts the ban, calling it unconstitutional and harmful to innovation.
- **2022**: Government imposes a flat 30% tax on crypto profits and 1% TDS on every transaction — without allowing loss deductions.
- **2023–2024**: Committees and working groups form to discuss regulation, but no clear law has emerged yet.

So, is crypto legal in India?

Yes, it is not banned — but it is taxed heavily and not regulated like traditional finance.

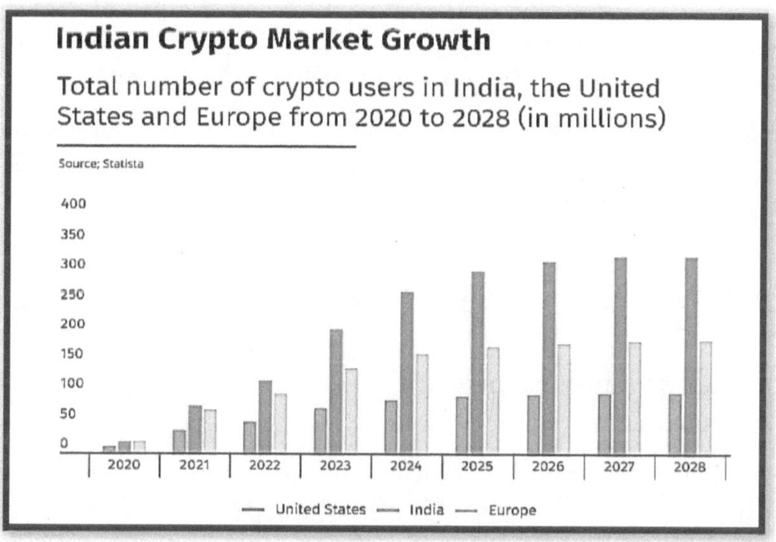

This regulatory grey area creates uncertainty for businesses and investors. Yet, the user base continues to grow, because the benefits are simply too powerful to ignore.

CHALLENGES THAT STILL EXIST

Crypto is not a magic wand. It comes with its own set of risks:

VOLATILITY

Crypto prices can crash or rise dramatically in a single day. This makes people nervous and prevents long-term use as a currency.

SCAMS AND FRAUD

Ponzi schemes, fake tokens, pump-and-dump groups — without regulation, many newcomers get duped.

LOW AWARENESS

Many still associate crypto with black money or the dark web. There is a huge need for education.

BANKING RESTRICTIONS

Some Indian banks still unofficially avoid supporting crypto platforms, making deposits and withdrawals hard for users.

A secure and thriving crypto environment needs strong regulation, investor protection, and public education.

BUILDERS, NOT JUST TRADERS

India is emerging not just as a crypto-using country, but a crypto-building one.

- ✓ Polygon (formerly Matic) is a globally recognized blockchain project built by Indian developers. It solves Ethereum's scaling issues and is widely used in DeFi and NFTs.

- ✓ Thousands of Indian developers are contributing to open-source crypto projects on GitHub.
- ✓ Events like ETHIndia, India Blockchain Week, and Web3 Conf are drawing massive participation.

This signals a cultural shift — from just speculating on coins to creating real technology and global solutions.

CRYPTO AND FINANCIAL INCLUSION

Crypto can be a great equalizer in India's deeply stratified financial ecosystem:

MICRO-INVESTING

Anyone with a phone and ₹100 can now invest in assets that were once for the elite.

DECENTRALIZED LENDING

Platforms like Aave or Compound allow users to borrow money using crypto as collateral — no credit score needed.

DIGITAL IDENTITY

Blockchain-based IDs can help the rural poor access banking, insurance, and welfare schemes without paperwork or corruption.

For many Indians left out by traditional systems, crypto offers access, dignity, and control.

THE ROLE OF WOMEN IN CRYPTO

For a long time, the world of cryptocurrency carried the reputation of being a male-dominated space — a playground for tech geeks, traders, and risk-takers who spoke in codes and numbers. Women were often missing from the conversation, not because they lacked ability, but because the doors to entry seemed intimidating and unwelcoming. But that perception is beginning to change, and the story of crypto is slowly becoming a story of inclusion.

- ✓ Platforms like *SheFi* and India-based communities are encouraging women to learn, invest, and build in Web3.
- ✓ Women creators are minting and selling NFTs, building DAOs (decentralized autonomous organizations), and educating others.
- ✓ Influencers like Nischal Shetty's team are creating inclusive products that invite female users to participate safely.

This inclusion is vital — because true financial empowerment includes everyone.

WHAT THE FUTURE MIGHT LOOK LIKE

Here's what India's crypto future could look like:

CBDC (CENTRAL BANK DIGITAL CURRENCY)

The RBI's digital rupee is in pilot stages and may soon be available nationwide. It brings the benefits of crypto with state backing.

SMART REGULATION

A well-thought law that encourages innovation while preventing fraud is on the horizon.

JOB CREATION

Web3 jobs — from crypto marketing to smart contract development — are increasing, even for non-tech roles.

EDUCATION REVOLUTION

Blockchain courses are entering Indian universities. Even YouTube and free online academies are educating the next generation.

India could become a global leader in decentralized tech — not just using the internet, but shaping its next phase.

Crypto in India is not a bubble or a passing trend. It's a reflection of what our economy needs: access, speed, transparency, and inclusion. From a small trader in Varanasi to a coder in Bangalore — the decentralized revolution is quietly transforming lives.

The government may take time to catch up. Institutions may resist. But the people — they are already onboard.

Whether you're a student, an entrepreneur, an artist, or a farmer — crypto gives you tools to build your financial future, your way.

In the decentralized world, you don't wait for permission — you create your own opportunity.

BITCOIN FOR BREAKFAST: CHAI AND CHANGE

It was a calm morning in Bengaluru. The air was fresh, and the street was slowly waking up. Raj, a young web developer, walked to his favorite chai shop. This was his daily routine — hot tea, fresh thoughts, and sometimes, a good chat.

The small café was run by Rohan, a young guy with big dreams. He had opened this café with his savings and a lot of hope. But Rohan was not just serving tea — he was also a big fan of crypto.

As Raj reached the counter, Rohan smiled.

"UPI or crypto today?" he asked with a playful grin.

Raj laughed. "Let's go with crypto. Let's start the day with the future!"

He opened a simple app on his phone, scanned a QR code, and sent a small Bitcoin payment. The whole thing was done in just two seconds.

No cash. No card. No bank. Just phone to phone.

"Payment received!" said Rohan, checking his screen.

Raj took his hot kulhad of chai and sat at a table nearby. He felt happy. This wasn't just tea — this was freedom. He was using money that no one could block, control, or delay.

AN OLD MAN, A QUESTION

At the next table sat an elderly uncle, sipping his tea and reading the newspaper. He had seen the payment happen and looked confused.

He leaned over and asked kindly, "Beta, what is this digital money? I don't understand it. It doesn't seem real. Can you trust it?"

Raj smiled. He liked questions. Especially from someone who was ready to listen.

"Uncle, do you use Paytm or Google Pay?" Raj asked.

"Yes, of course! Very easy. Even my milkman takes it now," replied the old man.

"Exactly. So, where is that money? Do you see it in your hand?"

The uncle thought for a moment. "No... it's in the bank app, I guess."

Raj nodded. "That's right. You already use digital money. The only difference is — your money in Paytm is controlled by banks and the government. But this one — Bitcoin — is not. You control it fully."

THE POWER OF CONTROL

Rohan, who was cleaning the counter, joined the conversation.

"Uncle, Bitcoin is like cash, but on your phone. You don't need permission from anyone to use it."

The uncle raised an eyebrow. "But is it safe? What if the price crashes? What if I lose my phone?"

Raj answered gently. "Yes, it's like gold. You have to be careful. But the value of Bitcoin has grown a lot over the years. And don't worry about losing your phone – your wallet can be backed up. You just need to learn how it works."

"Hmm... sounds new. And risky," the old man said.

"Everything new feels risky at first, uncle," Raj replied. "Remember when mobile phones first came? Or online banking? People were scared. Now everyone uses them."

A CAFÉ OF NEW IDEAS

All around the café, things were changing quietly:

- ✓ A delivery boy was watching a YouTube video on how to earn crypto through games.
- ✓ A college girl in the corner was learning about NFTs while sipping coffee.
- ✓ Rohan was planning to sell special coffee mugs as NFTs online.

Change was not just coming – it was already here, even in a small chai shop.

WHY BITCOIN MATTERS

Raj looked at his phone again. His wallet had just received another small payment from a foreign client. No bank, no delay, no fees.

He smiled. “This is why I love Bitcoin. It gives me control. It lets me work with anyone in the world without asking for permission.”

Rohan added, “It also helps people who can’t get bank accounts. Like small artists, gig workers, or villagers. Crypto is for everyone — not just the rich.”

The uncle listened quietly. Then he smiled a little.

“Maybe I don’t understand it fully, but I can see your passion. Maybe I’ll ask my grandson about it tonight,” he said.

Raj chuckled. “Do that, uncle. One day, you might pay for chai with Bitcoin too.”

THE REAL MEANING OF THIS MOMENT

As Raj finished his tea, he looked around. Everything seemed the same — same chairs, same chai, same road. But something was different.

A simple payment had started a new kind of conversation. A small café had become a window to the future. And tea was now more than just a drink — it was part of a quiet revolution.

The money didn’t need banks. The conversation didn’t need rules. And the change didn’t need anyone’s permission.

Bitcoin is not just about making profits. It’s about freedom, choice, and a new way to think about money. You don’t have to be an expert. You just have to be curious.

So, next time you sip your chai, ask yourself: Are you still using old money in a new world?

EARNING CRYPTO IN INDIA'S DIGITAL ECONOMY

Back home after his morning chai, Raj settled into his work desk, switched on his laptop, and logged into his favorite design software. Another exciting day as a freelance UI/UX designer awaited him. His first client today was from Dubai, seeking a sleek interface for a travel planning app. But unlike many others, Raj wasn't stressing over bank delays or high fees. He had already agreed to receive payment in Bitcoin.

This small decision was actually a big shift — not just for Raj, but for the entire Indian workforce. More and more Indians are now earning money directly in crypto, bypassing the old-school banking system altogether. What used to be just an investment tool or a trading buzzword is becoming an income source, a daily-use currency, and most importantly, a symbol of financial freedom.

WHY RAJ AND THOUSANDS LIKE HIM PREFER CRYPTO

When Raj began his freelance career a few years ago, he used the usual platforms: PayPal, Payoneer, international wire transfers. While functional, these systems came with many downsides:

- ✓ **SLOW TRANSFERS**: 3 to 7 business days, depending on the country.
- ✓ **HIGH CONVERSION FEES**: Losing 3-5% of income just in forex adjustments.
- ✓ **BANK INTERFERENCE**: Occasional freezes, limits, or sudden verification demands.
- ✓ **TIME ZONE ISSUES**: Delays caused by bank holidays or processing hours.

The experience was frustrating. Clients would pay on time, but the money would arrive late. Raj, like many others, felt trapped in a system designed for large corporations, not fast-moving freelancers.

Then he discovered crypto.

At first, he was cautious. But the first time he received payment in Bitcoin within minutes, with barely any transaction fee, he realized – this was the future of freelancing.

THE BIG BENEFITS OF CRYPTO FOR FREELANCERS

Let's break down the top reasons why Indian professionals are increasingly turning to crypto as a preferred method of earning:

INSTANT GLOBAL PAYMENTS

No more waiting for bank clearance. Bitcoin, Ethereum, USDT (a stablecoin) and other cryptocurrencies can be sent and received in real-time – even on weekends or public holidays.

Raj once received a payment from a U.S. client on a Sunday night – something that would've taken days with traditional banks.

VERY LOW FEES

Cross-border wire transfers can cost ₹500 to ₹2,000 per transaction. With crypto, sending money can cost as little as ₹5 to ₹10, especially using efficient networks like Polygon or Lightning Network.

For freelancers working on small gigs, this makes a huge difference.

BORDERLESS ACCESS

Banks often require country-specific rules and paperwork. Crypto wallets, on the other hand, are borderless. Whether your client is in Berlin or Bengaluru, payments move seamlessly.

This is especially useful for Indian remote workers serving clients in multiple countries.

FULL CONTROL OVER FUNDS

Traditional platforms can freeze accounts, hold money for weeks, or ask for endless verification. With crypto, you are the bank. Your wallet, your money, your rules.

Raj once faced a PayPal freeze for 21 days due to a flagged transaction. With crypto, that stress disappeared.

MORE OPTIONS, MORE FREEDOM

Crypto isn't just Bitcoin. There are stablecoins like USDT and USDC which are pegged to the U.S. dollar. These are great for freelancers who want to avoid volatility but still enjoy fast, global transfers.

Today, Raj accepts payment in USDT when he needs stability and uses Bitcoin or Ethereum for long-term holding.

India's Crypto Adoption Growth:

- 2020: ~5 million users
- 2023: ~25-30 million users
- 2025 (projected): 50+ million users

WHO'S EARNING IN CRYPTO?

Across India, a wide range of professionals are tapping into the crypto income wave:

- **Web developers and designers** working with international clients.
- **Content writers** for blockchain and tech platforms.
- **Digital marketers and SEO experts** serving crypto startups.
- **Video editors and animators** creating NFT ads and Web3 trailers.

- **Educators and YouTubers** offering blockchain-related content.
- **Bug bounty hunters and ethical hackers** contributing to blockchain security.
- **Blockchain developers** building DeFi apps, smart contracts, and token systems.

And here's the beauty: You don't need to be in Mumbai or Bangalore. Raj lives in Bengaluru, but many others earning in crypto live in places like Ranchi, Bhopal, Guwahati, and beyond.

HOW DO INDIANS CONVERT CRYPTO TO INR?

One common question is — what do people do after receiving crypto? Can they actually use it?

Absolutely. Here's how:

CRYPTO EXCHANGES

Apps like WazirX, CoinDCX, and Binance allow you to convert Bitcoin, Ethereum, or USDT into Indian Rupees instantly. The money gets deposited in your bank account.

PEER-TO-PEER (P2P) TRADING

You can directly sell your crypto to another person in exchange for bank transfer or UPI.

CRYPTO CARDS

Some global platforms offer debit cards that let you spend crypto like regular money (Note: not fully available in India yet, but coming soon).

Raj usually keeps 30% of his earnings in crypto for long-term holding and converts the rest to INR for expenses like rent, groceries, and savings.

THE BIGGER PICTURE: INDIA'S DIGITAL FREELANCE REVOLUTION

India has over 15 million freelancers, and the number is growing fast. With the rise of remote work and global gig platforms, Indian talent is now available to the entire world.

Crypto adds one powerful advantage: freedom from borders and banks.

Imagine:

- A graphic designer in Manipur working with a client in France.
- A blockchain writer in Surat publishing on a US blog.
- A smart contract developer in Pune contributing to a Canadian DAO.

All earning in crypto. All working without middlemen.

This is not just evolution. It's revolution.

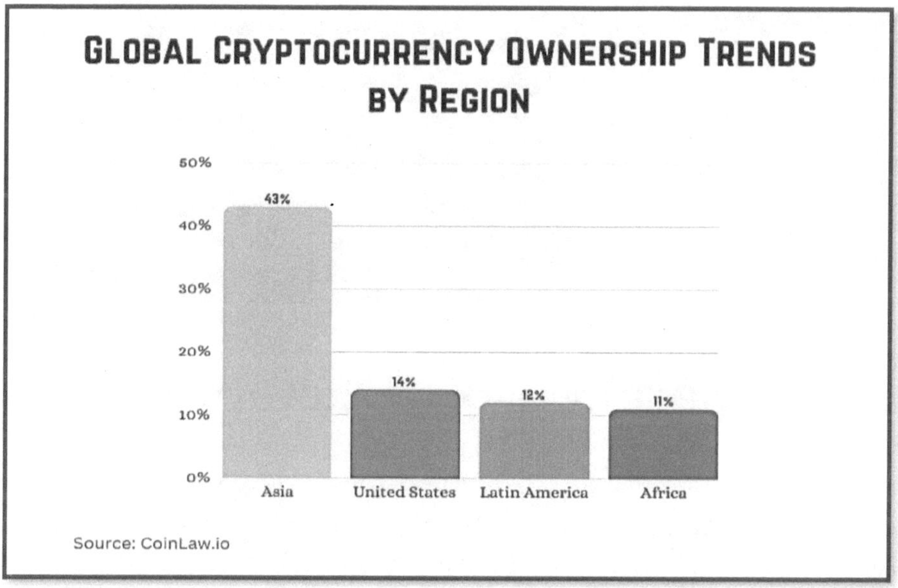

CHALLENGES TO WATCH OUT FOR

Of course, crypto isn't perfect. Freelancers should be aware of:

- **Volatility**: Prices can swing quickly. Use stablecoins when needed.
- **Regulations**: India taxes crypto gains. Be sure to report income correctly.
- **Scams and fake platforms**: Only use trusted wallets and exchanges.
- **Security**: Use two-factor authentication, hardware wallets, and never share private keys.

With a little caution and awareness, these risks can be easily managed.

CRYPTO TAX EQUATION IN INDIA

Tax Payable = (Total Profit from Crypto × 30%) + 4% Cess
Net Amount Received = Crypto Proceeds – Tax Payable – 1% TDS

FINAL THOUGHTS: A QUIET REVOLUTION IN MOTION

Back in his room, Raj submitted the final files to his client. Within minutes, he received the rest of his payment in Bitcoin. He smiled.

His work, his skills, his income — all flowing without borders.

In that moment, he wasn't just a freelancer. He was part of a silent revolution. A growing tribe of Indians who are embracing financial freedom, one crypto transaction at a time.

"Crypto is not just the future of money — it's the present of work."

And in India's digital economy, the smartest earners aren't just working harder — they're earning smarter.

P2P TRADING: THE INDIAN CRYPTO LIFELINE

Later in the afternoon, Raj opened his crypto apps — WazirX and Binance. These are two of the most popular platforms in India where people buy and sell cryptocurrencies. But Raj wasn't just checking prices. He was diving into P2P — or peer-to-peer — trading, something that had become increasingly popular in India.

After the Indian government introduced a 30% tax on crypto profits and added a 1% TDS (tax deducted at source) on every crypto transaction, many expected crypto trading to slow down. But what happened was the opposite — the crypto community adapted quickly.

Rather than give up, users found smarter ways to trade. P2P trading became a powerful alternative. In P2P, there's no centralized exchange holding your funds. Buyers and sellers connect directly, often using trusted platforms as an escrow. This means fewer intermediaries, faster access, and often fewer restrictions.

Raj's friend, Mehul, had been using P2P regularly. He explained the process:

"Bro, I hardly use banks now," Mehul said, sipping his cold coffee. "I buy USDT from a seller through P2P. I send it directly to my cousin in Canada. He converts it into Canadian dollars instantly. No SWIFT fees, no long waiting periods, no RBI documentation. It's instant."

What Mehul described wasn't just a cool hack. It was a revolution in how money moved — borderless, fast, and user-driven.

Across India, thousands of people had started using P2P platforms for various purposes:

- ✓ **Freelancers and remote workers** used P2P to receive payments in USDT or BTC and then convert it locally at better rates.
- ✓ **Students and families** used it to send money abroad quickly without going through the expensive, slow banking channels.
- ✓ **Crypto traders and enthusiasts** used it to bypass limitations or excessive charges placed by centralized exchanges.

What was fascinating was how this change wasn't limited to big cities. Even small towns like Bhopal, Ranchi, and Guwahati saw rising P2P activity. Young people with smartphones and basic crypto knowledge were now handling global payments with ease.

The government was cautious. They feared misuse, fraud, or illegal transactions. That's why they introduced the TDS rule — to monitor movement and collect data. But instead of blocking the space, it pushed people towards learning more about how to use crypto more privately and efficiently.

P2P had become a financial lifeline — especially in a country like India, where bureaucracy, currency conversion, and bank approvals often slow down progress.

For Raj and Mehul, this wasn't just a trend. It was freedom — freedom from slow systems, high fees, and red tape.

GAMING FOR CRYPTO: INDIA'S PLAY-TO-EARN BOOM

As evening approached, Raj decided to take a break. But instead of switching on Netflix or scrolling through social media, he logged into a play-to-earn (P2E) game.

Gaming had changed. It wasn't just for fun anymore. It had become a new way to earn income – especially for youth in India.

Raj had been playing crypto games for over a year. He'd made decent earnings in tokens and NFTs, which he could convert into rupees whenever needed.

Some of the platforms he explored included:

- **Axie Infinity**: A strategy-based game where players train and battle fantasy creatures called Axies. Winning battles earns you crypto tokens, which can be sold or used in-game.
- **The Sandbox and Decentraland**: Virtual worlds where users can buy digital land, build experiences, and earn from selling virtual assets.
- **Zed Run and Gods Unchained**: Games where owning digital assets (like horses or trading cards) becomes a source of income.
- **OpenSea**: The biggest NFT marketplace, where Indian artists, designers, and game players sell in-game items, art, and more for real income.

Play-to-earn wasn't just entertainment – it was a full-blown micro-economy.

In Mumbai, Raj had read about a group of college students who played P2E games daily and collectively earned enough to pay their semester fees. In places like Chennai and Pune, graphic designers who once worked for peanuts were now selling in-game assets and NFTs for thousands of rupees.

The barriers to entry were low. Anyone with a smartphone and some digital literacy could get started. Some platforms required initial investment, but many offered scholarship models – where investors lent their game assets to players in return for shared profits.

The best part? It taught young Indians about:

- Blockchain technology

- ❖ Crypto wallets and security
- ❖ Earning and saving in decentralized finance (DeFi)
- ❖ Digital ownership through NFTs

For a country with millions of gamers, crypto gaming had opened a new door — not just to money, but to tech education and independence.

Raj wasn't just playing games. He was building skills, earning crypto, and participating in a digital-first global economy.

MICRO INSIGHTS

Why Crypto is Popular in India

- ✓ Better returns compared to FDs and gold.
- ✓ No need for heavy documentation.
- ✓ Works 24/7 (unlike banks).

Risks

- ✓ Price volatility.
- ✓ Regulatory uncertainty.
- ✓ Security scams.

Opportunities

- ✓ Web3 jobs, blockchain startups, NFT creators.
- ✓ India's IT workforce shifting to decentralized projects.

A FUTURE BEYOND BORDERS

As the night settled, Raj took a moment to reflect. He sat on his balcony with a cup of tea, checking his crypto wallet on his phone.

His assets were safe. His Bitcoin held long-term value. His stablecoins like USDT and USDC were ready to be used for payments or saved for a rainy day. His gaming rewards were steadily growing, and freelance payments were no longer stuck in international bank pipelines.

It hit him — he wasn't just using crypto. He was living the future.

A few years ago, crypto seemed like a risky, niche idea. Something only tech geeks or risk-takers played with. Today, it was becoming part of India's digital lifestyle.

He had seen the journey:

- From Bitcoin being unknown to chaiwallahs accepting it.
- From banks warning users to now launching their own digital currencies (CBDCs).
- From parents doubting crypto to now asking their kids to teach them how it works.

He knew the road ahead wouldn't be easy. There would be:

- New tax rules
- Security concerns
- Market ups and downs
- Government crackdowns

But he also knew that the foundation had already been laid. Blockchain education was growing. Startups in crypto, DeFi, and NFTs were booming in India. Even traditional finance professionals were shifting toward Web3 roles.

And perhaps most importantly, the next generation was ready.

Kids today were growing up with an understanding of digital money. Teenagers were exploring NFTs and smart contracts. College students were earning through crypto gigs. The revolution wasn't being taught — it was being experienced.

Raj closed his laptop and looked at the sky. He felt something powerful.

"The financial revolution wasn't coming — it was already here."

And people like him were leading the way —. not with slogans or protests, but with code, creativity, and crypto.

From Bangalore to Bhopal, Mumbai to Manipur, a decentralized economy was taking root.
Slowly. Steadily. Unstoppable.

"The age of decentralized dreams has begun – and it belongs to all of us."

******

“The greatest revolution of the 21st century will not be technology itself, but how humans adapt their minds to live with it.”

*©Yuval Noah Harari (*Historian & Author of Homo Deus)*

CHAPTER TEN

THE PSYCHOLOGY OF DECENTRALIZATION – ARE HUMANS READY FOR FULL DIGITAL FREEDOM?

"Decentralization gives you power, but it also removes excuses. In this new world, your freedom and your failure are both your own."

– ***Balaji Srinivasan*** *(Former Coinbase CTO & Author)*

Varanasi, 2045

Aarav stands by the Ganges River, watching as worshippers dip their hands into the sacred waters. For centuries, India has balanced the old and the new, tradition and innovation.

But something feels different today.

His AI-powered news feed, linked to his decentralized social network, delivers the latest headlines:

- ❖ The Indian government has announced full integration of the Digital Rupee (CBDC) into all financial systems.
- ❖ A major cybersecurity breach has exposed the private keys of 500,000 users of a centralized exchange.
- ❖ A global DAO votes to form the world's first AI-run decentralized city, with no human leaders.

Aarav sighs. The world is changing faster than people can adapt.

For years, he has believed in decentralization, financial freedom, and Web3. But he has also seen friends lose money in crypto scams, struggle with the complexity of managing private keys, and even question whether a world without centralized institutions is too chaotic to function.

It raises an uncomfortable question:

Are humans psychologically ready for full decentralization?

Digital Freedom = (Self-Custody + Education) – Fear

THE PSYCHOLOGICAL SHIFT FROM CENTRALIZATION TO DECENTRALIZATION

For thousands of years, humans have relied on centralized institutions for security, stability, and governance.

- ✓ Governments provide laws, courts, and infrastructure.
- ✓ Banks store wealth, process transactions, and issue loans.
- ✓ Corporations offer jobs, manage payroll, and enforce contracts.

Most people have never questioned whether these institutions should exist.

Then, blockchain came along and said:

"You don't need banks. You don't need governments. You don't need middlemen. You can control everything yourself."

For many, this was exciting—but also terrifying.

WHY DO PEOPLE STRUGGLE WITH DECENTRALIZATION?

- **Responsibility** – If you lose your private keys, no one can help you.
- **Complexity** – Understanding smart contracts, wallets, and DeFi isn't easy.
- **Risk** – Without banks, there are no refunds, no customer service, no legal protections.
- **Fear of Change** – Most people are used to trusting institutions, not algorithms.

This shift requires a fundamental change in human psychology—from trusting centralized authorities to trusting code and themselves.

Are we ready for that?

THE PSYCHOLOGICAL BARRIERS TO FULL DECENTRALIZATION

Imagine a world where you don't need a bank account, a credit card, or even permission from anyone to move your money. No queues. No paperwork. No hidden fees. Just pure financial freedom.

Sounds liberating, right? But here's the twist — freedom comes with a heavy dose of responsibility.

In a decentralized system, *you* hold the keys — quite literally.

There are no bankers, no customer care helplines, no "forgot password" buttons. You are the bank.
And while that's empowering, it also terrifies many people.

Why? Because with great power comes great risk:

- ✓ Lose your private key? Your entire fortune vanishes. There's no "reset" option.
- ✓ Fall for a scam? Nobody's coming to save you. No chargebacks, no refunds.
- ✓ Send funds to the wrong wallet? Say goodbye. That money is gone forever.

$$\text{Risk Perception} = (\text{Lack of Knowledge})^2$$

For centuries, people have grown comfortable outsourcing financial safety to institutions — letting banks guard their savings and governments regulate fraud. But decentralization flips that model on its head. Suddenly, *you* are responsible for your own security.

This shift feels exciting for some but overwhelming for many. It's not just a technological challenge; it's a psychological one. People must unlearn old habits and embrace a world where trust moves from institutions to individuals.

And that's the real question: *Do people truly want full financial freedom if it means carrying the full weight of responsibility?*

Decentralization promises independence, but it also demands discipline. The future of finance isn't just about technology; it's about whether we are ready, mentally and emotionally, to be our own bank.

Key Points to Remember

Decentralization = Power + Responsibility
No intermediaries, but full accountability lies on the user.

Main Psychological Barriers

- ❖ Fear of losing private keys (no recovery like banks).
- ❖ Fear of scams & hacking.
- ❖ Lack of trust in technology over human institutions.
- ❖ Comfort in familiar systems (banks, governments).

Human Nature vs. Freedom

Many prefer convenience & security over self-sovereignty.

Digital Literacy Gap

Not everyone understands private keys, smart contracts, or cold wallets.

Generational Divide

Gen Z adapts faster to decentralization; older generations trust centralized systems.

REAL-WORLD EXAMPLE

In 2023, a man accidentally threw away a hard drive containing 8,000 Bitcoin, worth over $200 million.

Would the average person be comfortable with this level of responsibility?

Many still prefer banks, customer support, and safety nets—even if it means giving up control.

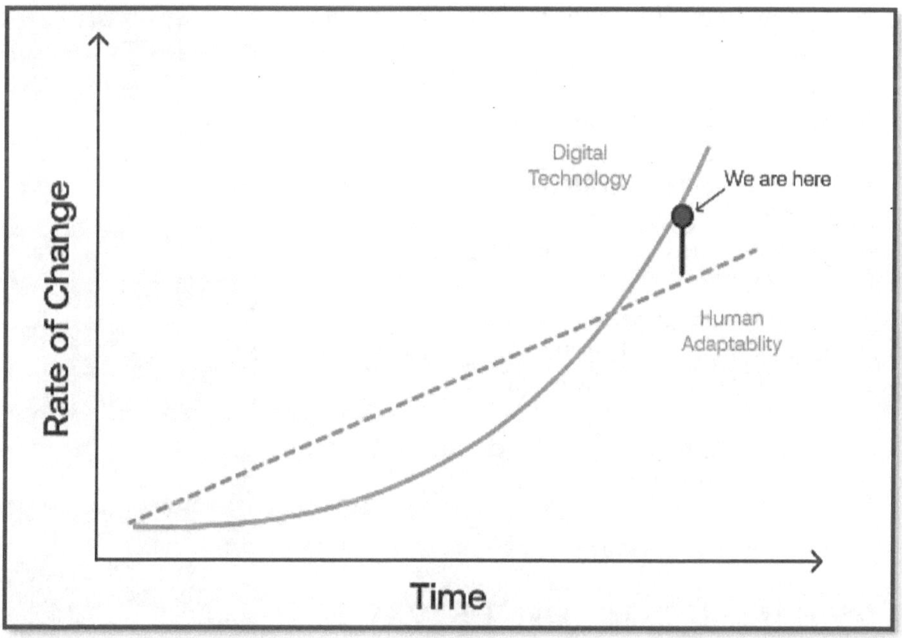

FEAR OF CHAOS – CAN THE WORLD FUNCTION WITHOUT CENTRALIZED GOVERNMENTS?

Many Web3 idealists believe the world doesn't need politicians, governments, or bureaucracies.

Instead, DAOs (Decentralized Autonomous Organizations) and smart contracts can manage everything.

BUT WHAT HAPPENS WHEN LAWS NEED TO CHANGE?

- ✓ Who decides what's legal and what isn't?
- ✓ How do decentralized societies handle crime, disputes, and public services?
- ✓ Can AI and smart contracts replace human judgment?

REAL-WORLD EXAMPLE

El Salvador adopted Bitcoin as legal tender in 2021. But when prices crashed, people panicked—many still wanted government safety nets.

Would people really trust DAOs to manage laws, justice, and economies?

Or would they eventually demand central authorities return?

THE ILLUSION OF PRIVACY – CAN WE TRULY ESCAPE SURVEILLANCE?

One of the biggest promises of decentralization is privacy and financial freedom.

But is that realistic?

Governments are already trying to track, regulate, and control crypto transactions.

Mini Definitions

PRIVATE KEY

Your digital signature to access crypto. Lose it = lose funds.

SELF-CUSTODY

Holding your own assets without relying on banks or exchanges.

DEFI

Decentralized Finance; finance without banks, using smart contracts.

COLD WALLET

Offline crypto storage for security.

- ❖ CBDCs (Central Bank Digital Currencies) will allow full government surveillance.
- ❖ AI-powered financial tracking will detect tax evasion and anonymous transactions.
- ❖ Many DeFi platforms are being forced to comply with KYC (Know Your Customer) regulations.

REAL-WORLD EXAMPLE

- ✓ China's Digital Yuan (CBDC) lets the government track every citizen's spending in real time.
- ✓ The U.S. is considering a "crypto tax reporting" law, forcing all transactions to be monitored.

Will decentralization truly provide privacy, or will it be overregulated by governments?

THE TWO TYPES OF PEOPLE IN THE DECENTRALIZED WORLD

As decentralization spreads, two groups of people will emerge:

THE ADAPTORS – THOSE WHO EMBRACE FULL DIGITAL FREEDOM

These are people who:

- ✓ Learn how to use hardware wallets & private keys securely.
- ✓ Participate in DAOs, earning income from Web3 communities.
- ✓ Use decentralized services for finance, governance, and social media.

They thrive in this new world because they accept full control over their money, identity, and decisions.

THE DEPENDENTS – THOSE WHO STILL NEED CENTRALIZED SYSTEMS

These are people who:

- ✓ Prefer banks, customer support, and financial safety nets.
- ✓ Feel overwhelmed by crypto, wallets, and smart contracts.
- ✓ Trust governments to handle governance, laws, and economies.

They may still use crypto and blockchain technology, but they want a balance—some decentralization, but also some centralized oversight.

Aspect	Centralized Mindset	Decentralized Mindset
Security Belief	Trust banks & insurance	Trust personal security
Responsibility	Outsourced to institutions	100% user-controlled
Recovery	Bank refunds, help desks	No recovery if keys lost
Privacy	Data shared with authorities	Self-owned, anonymous

THE FUTURE: A HYBRID SYSTEM OF CENTRALIZATION & DECENTRALIZATION

Most experts agree that:

The world won't be 100% decentralized.
But it also won't be 100% centralized anymore.

Instead, we will have a hybrid system where:

- ✓ DeFi exists alongside regulated banks.
- ✓ DAOs & AI-driven governance manage some aspects of society.
- ✓ Governments regulate blockchain, but don't control it entirely.

This middle path ensures that people have choice, flexibility, and security.

But the real question is:

Will people actively fight for decentralization, or will they choose comfort over freedom?

2050: A DAY IN A PARTIALLY DECENTRALIZED WORLD

- ❖ ***7:00 AM*** – Aarav checks his investments, which are fully managed by AI-driven smart contracts.
- ❖ ***10:00 AM*** – He pays his rent in stablecoins, but it's recorded on a government-approved blockchain.
- ❖ ***1:00 PM*** – His reputation score (stored on a decentralized identity system) lets him apply for a DeFi loan instantly.

- ❖ ***4:00 PM*** – He attends a virtual governance meeting, where citizens vote on new policies via blockchain.
- ❖ ***8:00 PM*** – His self-driving electric taxi automatically pays for charging using a blockchain-based smart contract.

Aarav enjoys both freedom and security.

The world isn't fully decentralized.

But it's not fully controlled either.

It's somewhere in between.

And maybe that's the best outcome.

"Decentralization isn't just a technology shift; it's a mindset shift. Freedom demands courage."

******

❝

"The internet is not going away. Blockchain is not going away. The question is whether we want to embrace this technology early and shape it for good, or wait until it shapes us."

@Vitalik Buterin
(Ethereum Co-founder)

CHAPTER ELEVEN

WHAT'S NEXT? PREPARING FOR THE DECENTRALIZED FUTURE

> *Decentralization is not just a technology shift; it is a civilization shift."*
>
> *– Balaji Srinivasan*

Mumbai, 2055,

Aarav steps onto the rooftop of his solar-powered smart home overlooking the Arabian Sea. His AI assistant updates him on his finances.

- ✓ His crypto wallet has grown by 12% overnight, thanks to AI-powered DeFi investments.

- ✓ His metaverse real estate is generating passive income, as virtual office spaces are leased out to companies worldwide.
- ✓ His reputation score has increased, allowing him to access new global work opportunities—no resume needed.

He no longer worries about bank failures, inflation, or government regulations restricting his money.

Aarav has full financial freedom, borderless work opportunities, and self-sovereign identity.

But as he looks at the skyline of Mumbai, now a mix of futuristic smart buildings and remnants of the old economy, he knows that not everyone has adapted.

Many people still rely on the government for financial aid. Others struggle with the shift to digital economies. And some nations still resist decentralization, trying to control their citizens through CBDCs, social credit systems, and surveillance technologies.

The world isn't fully decentralized yet.

But it's clear:

Decentralization is not a possibility anymore—it's an inevitability.

The only question that remains is:

How do we prepare for it?

THE KEY SKILLS & KNOWLEDGE FOR THE DECENTRALIZED FUTURE

If decentralization is the future, then what should we learn today to succeed in this new world?

FINANCIAL LITERACY IN A CRYPTO-FIRST ECONOMY

In the traditional world, financial literacy meant understanding banks, loans, and stocks.

In a decentralized world, it means:

- ❖ Knowing how to store, trade, and secure crypto assets.
- ❖ Understanding how DeFi lending, staking, and yield farming work.
- ❖ Learning to invest in tokenized assets like digital real estate, DAOs, and NFTs.

HOW TO PREPARE?

- ✓ Take online courses on DeFi & crypto investing.
- ✓ Use blockchain wallets instead of traditional banks sometimes.
- ✓ Experiment with earning through DeFi platforms.
- ✓ Key Platforms to Watch: Binance, Uniswap, AAVE, Curve, Metamask

SKILLS FOR AI & WEB3 CAREERS

The world of work is changing faster than ever before. Automation and Artificial Intelligence are no longer distant possibilities — they are realities reshaping industries today. From factories to finance, machines and algorithms are replacing routine, repetitive jobs at lightning speed.

But here's the good news: while some doors are closing, entirely new ones are opening. And many of those doors lead straight into the world of Web3 and decentralized economies.

In this emerging landscape, skills are not just about surviving — they are about thriving in a future where technology and creativity go hand in hand. The jobs of tomorrow will not look like the jobs of today. Instead of climbing traditional career ladders, people will be building, innovating, and collaborating in borderless digital ecosystems.

In the age of AI and Web3, your greatest skill will be the ability to learn, unlearn, and relearn as technology evolves. Unlike traditional industries, this new economy isn't limited by geography or old hierarchies — it rewards innovation, passion, and the courage to step into uncharted territory.

The question isn't whether jobs will change. They already are.

The real question is: *Will you be ready with the skills that shape the future instead of being left behind by it?*

HIGH-DEMAND SKILLS FOR THE FUTURE

- **BLOCKCHAIN DEVELOPMENT** – Smart contracts, Solidity, Rust.
- **NFT & METAVERSE DESIGN** – Digital art, 3D modeling, VR creation
- **AI & MACHINE LEARNING** – AI-driven automation, chatbot development
- **DECENTRALIZED BUSINESS STRATEGY** – DAO management, tokenomics, governance
- **CONTENT CREATION & DIGITAL INFLUENCE** – Metaverse influencers, NFT marketing

HOW TO PREPARE?

- ✓ Learn coding (Solidity, Python, Rust).

- ✓ Start a Web3 career on platforms like Mirror, Zora, or Lens Protocol.
- ✓ Explore Play-to-Earn gaming, Metaverse design, and AI-powered content creation.

HOW BECOME A DIGITAL CITIZEN OF THE FUTURE

For centuries, your citizenship was a matter of chance — decided by the soil you were born on or the borders your parents belonged to. A passport, a flag, and a national identity defined who you were in the eyes of the world.

But the 21st century is rewriting that story. In the age of decentralization, citizenship is no longer limited by geography. It is becoming a choice.

Imagine a world where instead of being bound to one nation, you could align yourself with a smart city built on blockchain, a virtual nation powered by decentralized governance, or even a global digital economy that transcends borders. This isn't science fiction — it's already unfolding.

Blockchain-based nations and DAOs are offering digital passports, virtual residency, and access to borderless opportunities.

People are beginning to ask:

SHORT NOTES (Mini Definitions for Quick Recall)

DAO (Decentralized Autonomous Organization): A digital community with shared rules and treasury on blockchain.

CBDC (Central Bank Digital Currency): A centralized government-backed digital rupee.

Interoperability: Different blockchains working seamlessly together.

Metaverse Economy: Virtual world jobs, digital goods, and immersive commerce powered by blockchain.

Why should my identity and rights be tied to one government when technology allows me to connect, work, and earn anywhere in the world?

Becoming a digital citizen of the future means more than just holding a crypto wallet. It means:

- ✓ **Voting in DAOs** that govern digital communities.
- ✓ **Earning and spending** in cryptocurrencies that aren't tied to any one country.
- ✓ **Owning digital assets** like NFTs and virtual land that prove your place in this new society.
- ✓ **Choosing your nation** not by birth, but by belief — in transparency, freedom, and decentralization.

The passport of tomorrow won't just be a government-issued booklet. It could be your blockchain identity — a secure, tamper-proof record that carries your reputation, your assets, and your rights across both physical and digital worlds.

In this future, citizenship is no longer about where you're from. It's about where you belong.

NEW OPPORTUNITIES

- ❖ Remote work for global DAOs – No need for visas, just blockchain-based reputation.
- ❖ Joining blockchain-powered smart cities – No traditional governance, only decentralized systems.
- ❖ Using blockchain-based identity & reputation systems – No passports, just global verification.

HOW TO PREPARE?

- ✓ Build an on-chain reputation by working with DAOs.

✓ Create an AI-managed digital identity (like Worldcoin, Proof-of-Humanity).

✓ Explore blockchain-based citizenship models in smart cities like Prospera, Culdesac, and Bitcoin City.

Wealth in Web3 = Early Adoption + Consistency – Fear

SECURING WEALTH & PRIVACY IN A FULLY DIGITAL WORLD

The future of money is digital. Around the globe, economies are rapidly moving toward blockchain-powered systems, where every transaction can be tracked in real time. On the surface, this looks efficient, transparent, and progressive. But behind the shine lies a deeper question — in a world where everything is digital, will individuals still be able to protect their wealth and their privacy?

Governments are already preparing for this new reality. Central Bank Digital Currencies (CBDCs) are being launched as the "official" digital versions of national currencies. They promise faster payments, easy cross-border transactions, and a financial system that operates at the speed of the internet. Alongside, digital IDs are being linked with financial services to create a seamless ecosystem.

But here's the catch — these systems also allow governments to watch every transaction you make. From the cup of tea you buy at the corner shop to the amount you donate to a cause, every move could be logged, analyzed, and even controlled. Imagine a future where spending could be restricted by rules, or where "non-compliant" citizens find their accounts frozen with a single click.

This is where blockchain's true spirit comes in. While CBDCs represent centralized digital money, decentralized cryptocurrencies like Bitcoin and Ethereum offer something different — freedom and privacy. They allow individuals to hold their wealth in wallets only they can access, without the need for banks or middlemen. They create a parallel economy where people, not institutions, set the rules.

Protecting wealth in such a digital-first world will not just mean owning assets, but also owning knowledge. People will need to understand private keys, cold wallets, and the importance of digital security. Privacy tools, decentralized exchanges, and anonymous transactions will become as valuable as gold once was.

The future, then, is a battle of choices. Do we allow complete surveillance in the name of convenience? Or do we build a parallel path where individuals can truly secure both their wealth and their freedom? The answer will decide whether the digital revolution empowers humanity — or controls it.

HOW TO MAINTAIN PRIVACY & FINANCIAL FREEDOM?

- ❖ Use decentralized wallets – Store assets in non-custodial wallets like Ledger or Trezor.
- ❖ Use privacy coins – Monero, Zcash, and Tornado Cash help protect transactions.
- ❖ Diversify assets – Own a mix of Bitcoin, stablecoins, tokenized real estate, and AI-driven investments.

HOW TO PREPARE?

- ✓ Learn to use decentralized exchanges (DEXs) instead of traditional banks.
- ✓ Understand how privacy-focused DeFi works.
- ✓ Keep assets in multiple crypto wallets for safety.

THE ROLE OF GOVERNMENTS IN THE DECENTRALIZED WORLD

It's tempting to imagine that in a fully decentralized future, governments will simply fade away — replaced by algorithms, DAOs, and borderless blockchain communities. But history tells us something different: power doesn't vanish, it adapts.

Even in the age of digital freedom, governments will not disappear. Instead, they will evolve into hybrid systems — blending the authority of traditional nation-states with the transparency, efficiency, and inclusivity of blockchain.

These future-ready governments may look very different from today's bureaucratic giants.

Imagine a world where:

- ✓ Transparent governance and voting happen on blockchain, making fraud and manipulation almost impossible. Every citizen can verify their vote; every policy decision is visible on a public ledger.
- ✓ AI-driven policies are crafted not on outdated statistics but on real-time economic data flowing in from millions of transactions across a digital economy. Taxation, welfare, and infrastructure planning become dynamic, responsive, and data-accurate.
- ✓ Legal structures for DAOs and digital citizens emerge, giving people the freedom to belong to both physical nations and digital communities. A person in India could also be a registered citizen of a blockchain-powered city in the metaverse — with rights, responsibilities, and protections in both worlds.

Instead of clashing with decentralization, forward-thinking governments will integrate with it. They will act less like rulers and more like facilitators — ensuring security, fairness, and accountability while allowing innovation to flourish.

This doesn't mean the journey will be smooth. Power struggles, regulations, and conflicts between old systems and new models are inevitable. But as governments transform, one thing becomes clear:

The future of governance will not be about control, but about collaboration between people, technology, and policy.

In the decentralized world, the role of governments won't be to hold people back — it will be to help them move forward.

Decentralized Growth = (Community Strength) ² ÷ Dependence on Central Authorities

THE FUTURE OF INDIA'S GOVERNANCE (2055 VISION)

- Smart Contracts Replace Government Paperwork – Land records, licenses, and contracts run automatically on blockchain.
- Decentralized Voting Systems – Citizens vote directly on policies via blockchain, reducing corruption.
- Crypto-Based Taxation – Taxes are collected via smart contracts, ensuring fairness & transparency.

Governments that embrace decentralization will thrive.

Governments that fight it will be left behind.

2035–2055: THE TIMELINE OF DECENTRALIZATION

📅 2035

DeFi replaces traditional banks for loans, savings, and investments.
Metaverse jobs & AI-powered DAOs create borderless employment.

📅 2040

Major cities transition into blockchain-powered smart economies.
Crypto becomes the dominant global currency for international trade.

📅 2045

Education is fully decentralized, with AI tutors & blockchain-based certification.
Physical cash is nearly extinct; digital wallets are universal.

📅 2050

Smart cities operate as independent blockchain-based economies.
The world has a hybrid governance system—part AI, part decentralized DAOs.

📅 2055

People live in a fully decentralized society, with AI-driven finance, governance, and economies.

> **Future Readiness (FR)** = Digital Literacy × Adaptability × Security Awareness

FINAL THOUGHTS: WILL YOU ADAPT OR BE LEFT BEHIND?

Decentralization is more than just Bitcoin, DeFi apps, or smart contracts. It represents something much larger — a transformation of human freedom and opportunity. It is about shifting power away from traditional gatekeepers and placing it directly in the hands of individuals.

For centuries, institutions-controlled money, information, and governance. Now, technology has given us the tools to rewrite that story. The question is no longer whether decentralization will happen — it already has. From cross-border crypto payments to blockchain-powered communities, the revolution is unfolding around us every single day.

In this new world, *adaptation is survival.*

- ✓ Those who embrace change will find new careers, new wealth, and new forms of empowerment.
- ✓ Those who resist will find themselves left behind, clinging to a system that no longer works in a borderless digital era.

The decentralized future is not a distant dream. It is here, quietly reshaping economies, cities, and identities. And it is unstoppable.

So, the real question you must ask yourself is simple yet profound:

Will you adapt, evolve, and thrive in this new era — or be left behind in the shadows of the old world?

The story of the future is now in your hands — quite literally, in your private keys, your wallets, and your choices.

The world is changing.

The power is shifting.

The time to act is now.

Action Plan

Educate Yourself Continuously
Join online courses, read crypto-native blogs, and experiment with dApps.

Build a Web3 Wallet
Start with small transactions; learn the process of storing keys and using decentralized exchanges.

Explore Opportunities

- ✓ Freelancing in crypto projects.
- ✓ Investing small amounts in Bitcoin, Ethereum, or Indian Web3 startups.
- ✓ Learning smart contract programming (Solidity, Rust).

Secure Your Digital Future

- ✓ Use hardware wallets.
- ✓ Enable 2FA & never share seed phrases.
- ✓ Stay updated on scams & hacks.

Think Globally, Act Locally

- ✓ Join Indian crypto communities.
- ✓ Collaborate with international Web3 projects.

The decentralized future won't wait. Those who prepare today will own tomorrow.

******

"True decentralization will not be achieved by technology alone, but by the collective courage of humanity to trust itself more than its rulers."

@Growmoneyinfo

CHAPTER TWELVE

THE FINAL STEP– CAN HUMANITY ACHIEVE FULL DECENTRALIZATION ?

"Decentralization is not the end of authority; it is the beginning of responsibility."

– Balaji Srinivasan

Varanasi, 2050,

On the banks of the Ganges, in one of the world's oldest cities, an ancient ritual takes place. A group of monk's chant mantras as the river flows endlessly, unchanged for millennia.

Yet, around them, everything else has changed.

- Digital identities stored on blockchain have replaced paper documents.
- AI-powered governance has eliminated bureaucracy and corruption.
- Cryptocurrencies have rendered traditional banks obsolete.
- Smart contracts have replaced legal systems, ensuring fairness without courts.

This is not the future. This is the present.

Humanity has arrived at the final stage of decentralization—a world where power is no longer controlled by a select few but is distributed among all.

But is this really the utopia that early blockchain pioneers envisioned?

Or has decentralization created new challenges that no one anticipated?

WHAT DOES FULL DECENTRALIZATION LOOK LIKE?

Imagine waking up in 2050. The world you see is nothing like the one your grandparents lived in. The governments, banks, and corporations that once dictated every aspect of human life have lost their monopoly on power. Centralized authority is no longer the center of gravity. Humanity has shifted — not through revolution in the streets, but through evolution in the code.

No longer tied to fragile paper notes or inflation-ridden national currencies, money now lives on blockchains. Bitcoin, Ethereum, and other decentralized assets form the backbone of global exchange. A farmer in Kenya sells produce in Bitcoin to a trader in India. A musician in Mexico gets paid in stablecoins by fans in Germany. Governments can no longer print their way out of debt or manipulate value. For the first time in history, people trust math over ministers.

Your passport no longer defines who you are. Instead, digital identities stored on decentralized blockchains allow you to carry your credentials, achievements, and reputation anywhere. No nation owns you. No bureaucracy controls your access. With one click, you prove who you are—secure, private, and borderless. From education certificates to medical records, everything belongs to you and only you.

The 9-to-5 office, the corporate ladder, the cubicle—these are relics of the past. Instead, DAOs (Decentralized Autonomous Organizations) and Metaverse economies dominate. A designer in Kolkata collaborates with a coder in Lagos and a strategist in São Paulo, all paid in crypto, all voting on decisions equally. There's no CEO, no HR, no boss. People don't "work for" organizations anymore—they *work with them*. The global job market has flattened into one vast, permissionless ecosystem.

Political systems once plagued by corruption and inefficiency are being replaced with blockchain-based voting and AI-assisted policymaking. Imagine a world where elections are instant, transparent, and immune to fraud. Where policies adjust dynamically based on real-time data—healthcare budgets rise automatically during pandemics, and tax relief flows instantly after natural disasters. Governance becomes less about promises and more about proof.

This vision may sound like a fantasy. But it isn't. Pieces of it are already unfolding. Estonia has built digital ID systems. India is experimenting with blockchain in governance. DAOs manage billions in assets. Nations are adopting Bitcoin as legal tender. Slowly but steadily, the decentralized reality is coming alive.

By 2050, parts of this reality are already alive. From digital nations to borderless currencies, from decentralized jobs to AI-powered governance, humanity is slowly stepping into its most radical chapter yet: a world where power no longer flows top-down, but outwards—to everyone.

KEY PILLARS OF A FULLY DECENTRALIZED SOCIETY

A decentralized world cannot run on technology alone. For it to stand strong, it needs clear foundations—principles that guide how people live, work, trade, and trust each other without central authorities. These are the pillars that hold the system together, ensuring freedom does not slip into chaos, and equality does not get lost in complexity.

DECENTRALIZED MONEY (THE END OF FIAT CURRENCY?)

Traditional money—rupees, dollars, euros—was always controlled by governments and central banks.

But in a fully decentralized world:

- Bitcoin and stablecoins become the standard currency for global trade.
- People transact directly with smart wallets, eliminating banks completely.
- National currencies fade, replaced by community-driven digital assets.

REAL-WORLD EXAMPLE (India, 2050)

The streets of Jaipur buzz with life. Tourists bargain for colorful textiles, while locals buy spices and street food. But there's no sound of cash exchanging hands—no rustle of rupee notes, no swipe of plastic cards. Every vendor, from the tea seller on the corner to the jeweler in the market, accepts payments in Digital Rupees or Bitcoin with a simple scan. Transactions happen in seconds, secure and effortless.

Beyond the markets, the shift is even bigger. India no longer depends on the U.S. dollar for international trade. When India imports soybeans from Brazil or exports software services, the payments move through stablecoin settlements. No banks, no paperwork, no waiting. Just instant, transparent transfers between nations.

What once took days of clearance and layers of bureaucracy now happens in moments. Money has become borderless, and trade flows like electricity—fast, invisible, and unstoppable.

DECENTRALIZATION = TRUST IN CODE + COLLECTIVE CONSENSUS - CENTRAL AUTHORITY

SELF-SOVEREIGN IDENTITY (NO MORE GOVERNMENT-ISSUED IDS?)

For centuries, governments-controlled identities, passports, and citizenship.

In a decentralized world:

- ✓ Every person owns their own digital identity on a blockchain.

✓ Passports & citizenships are replaced by global reputation scores.

✓ AI verifies identities instantly, removing the need for physical IDs.

REAL-WORLD EXAMPLE (Varanasi, 2050)

The ghats of Varanasi glow with neon holograms as the ancient city blends seamlessly with futuristic tech. Aarav, now 50, strolls through the bustling streets, his blockchain-based global ID stored securely in his smart lens. With it, he travels across smart cities visa-free, never worrying about passports, borders, or paperwork.

Gone are the days of plastic cards and paper documents. Aarav doesn't carry a driver's license anymore. Instead, he relies on an AI-powered mobility pass linked to his identity on the blockchain. With a simple blink command, the system summons a sleek self-driving taxi, doors opening automatically as it verifies his credentials.

In seconds, Aarav is on his way, gliding past temples and digital billboards. The city's AI traffic grid syncs with his pass, ensuring zero delays and personalized routes. For Aarav, moving between worlds—physical, digital, and cultural—has become as effortless as breathing.

THE METAVERSE GOVERNMENT (NO MORE POLITICIANS?)

What if governments no longer made decisions for people?

In a fully decentralized world:

✓ Citizens vote on policies through blockchain-based DAOs.

✓ Smart contracts execute laws automatically, preventing corruption.

✓ AI-driven governance makes real-time decisions, based on transparent data.

REAL-WORLD EXAMPLE (BANGALORE, 2050)

Bangalore, once known as India's tech capital, has transformed into a model of decentralized governance. Here, no one files tax returns or waits for government officials. Instead, every transaction Aarav makes—his salary, his investments, even his daily coffee—flows directly through the blockchain. Taxes are calculated and collected automatically, without a single form or delay.

On the other side, the city's public funds are distributed with total transparency. Citizens can open a public ledger and see exactly where every rupee goes—whether it's building a new solar grid, upgrading hospitals, or maintaining smart roads. Nothing is hidden; nothing is lost.

The old world of lobbying, political parties, and backroom deals has disappeared. Decisions are made by decentralized community councils, powered by blockchain voting. People don't place their trust in politicians—they place it in transparent code.

In Bangalore, 2050, governance isn't a struggle for power. It's a shared system where technology ensures fairness, accountability, and trust.

AI-DRIVEN WORK & EDUCATION (NO MORE BOSSES OR SCHOOLS?)

The traditional job market is gone.

Instead of applying for jobs at companies, people work for decentralized AI-powered DAOs.

Education is no longer controlled by institutions.

Instead:

- ✓ Students learn through blockchain-based AI tutors.
- ✓ Degrees are replaced by NFT-certified skills.
- ✓ People work from anywhere in the world, earning in crypto.

REAL-WORLD EXAMPLE (DELHI, 2050)

In a co-living hub in Delhi, a 19-year-old student from Chennai sits by her smart desk. She's not enrolled in any university, nor does she carry piles of textbooks. Instead, she learns AI programming through a decentralized education platform, where lessons flow from experts across the globe. Every skill she masters is stamped with a blockchain-verified certificate, impossible to fake, recognized everywhere.

The moment she completes her course; she doesn't send out résumés or knock on company doors. Instead, her profile is instantly matched with a global DAO—a decentralized organization working on AI-driven medical systems. Within hours, she's contributing code that will help doctors diagnose patients in Africa, Asia, and beyond.

There's no boss watching her, no office walls surrounding her, no time clock dictating her hours. Her only boundaries are her creativity and ambition. She works, she earns, and she grows—on her own terms.

For her, freedom isn't just an idea. It's the way she lives, every single day.

DIGITAL REAL ESTATE & SMART CITIES (A WORLD WITHOUT BORDERS?)

What happens when people are no longer tied to nations?

In a fully decentralized world:

- ✓ Anyone can buy real estate in any country using tokenized assets.
- ✓ Smart cities operate as independent, blockchain-powered economies.
- ✓ People choose which city to live in based on economic and social values.

REAL-WORLD EXAMPLE (DUBAI, 2050)

Dubai's skyline glitters like a jewel of the future. The city hums with energy, not just from its towers and flying pods, but from the people who now call it home—digital nomads from India, Singapore, Europe, and beyond. They aren't bound by passports or national borders anymore. Instead, they belong to blockchain-powered smart cities, where identity, income, and community all live on the chain.

Here, taxes are no longer enforced but chosen. Citizens contribute voluntarily through DAO-based governance, where every rupee, dirham, or bitcoin is allocated openly on transparent ledgers. People don't complain about corruption because there is none—the system itself is incorruptible.

For the first time in human history, nations are not accidents of birth. People can now choose their digital nation, aligning with communities that share their values, goals, and dreams. A coder in Mumbai might pledge allegiance to a Health DAO, while an artist from Paris joins a Creativity DAO—each citizen building a future not by borders, but by belief.

Dubai, 2050, is no longer just a city. It's a living prototype of borderless freedom, where identity is digital, governance is decentralized, and belonging is a choice, not a destiny.

THE CHALLENGES OF FULL DECENTRALIZATION

A fully decentralized world sounds like a dream—no corrupt leaders, no greedy banks, no borders holding people back. Everything runs on open code, transparent ledgers, and community power.

But every dream has its shadows. When power shifts from governments to code, new problems appear. What happens if the code itself breaks? Who keeps people safe when there's no central police? And how do we care for the millions who cannot adapt to such a fast-changing world?

Decentralization gives us freedom, but freedom without structure can also create confusion, inequality, and chaos. To build a better future, we need to face these challenges head-on.

WHO FIXES MISTAKES?

In a world run by code, even the smallest error can cause chaos. A single flaw in a smart contract might drain millions overnight. But who steps in then? If an AI-driven DAO collapses, leaving thousands without pay, who takes the blame—an algorithm, or the people who trusted it?

Decentralization promises freedom, but it also raises a haunting question:

Who is accountable when the system itself fails?

HOW DO YOU MAINTAIN LAW & ORDER?

If governments fade and everything is decentralized, how do we stop crime? Who hunts down digital thieves when wallets are hacked or fraud runs wild? Without a central police force, can cities truly guarantee safety—or will security itself become a service run by private DAOs? A decentralized future may remove corruption, but it could also create a jungle where only the smartest survive.

WHAT HAPPENS TO THOSE LEFT BEHIND?

Not everyone can instantly adapt to a blockchain-powered world. Millions still depend on traditional jobs, pensions, or government aid. But in a system where the safety nets vanish, who protects the vulnerable? Will the elderly, the poor, and the digitally illiterate be forgotten? Decentralization may break chains of corruption, but it also risks cutting away the lifelines that many depend on.

The dream of a fully decentralized future shines bright, but beneath the glow lies a darker truth: freedom without structure comes with its own shadows.

HOW TO HANDLE THE CHALLENGES OF FULL DECENTRALIZATION

Decentralization is powerful, but it is not perfect. If we want this system to truly work for everyone, we must learn how to deal with its weak spots—mistakes in code, law and order without a central force, and the risk of leaving vulnerable people behind.

The good news is, these problems are not impossible to solve. With smart design, creative thinking, and a culture of care, we can build a decentralized world that is not only free, but also safe, fair, and humane.

WHEN CODE FAILS: FIXING MISTAKES WITHOUT A BOSS

In a world where code runs everything, even a small bug can create a big disaster. So, we need safety brakes in every important smart contract—just like airplanes have emergency systems. If money starts flowing the wrong way, the system can pause automatically, giving people time to react before it's too late.

No single person should control this pause. Instead, it should be unlocked by a group of guardians—community councils, independent auditors, and watchdog groups across the world.

Also, every piece of important code must be tested again and again by both AI and human experts. If they miss something, they lose reputation and rewards. And if something still goes wrong, there should be a rescue fund ready to pay victims instantly, so people don't suffer while debates drag on.

The key idea:

Decentralization doesn't mean mistakes can't be fixed—it means mistakes are fixed together, openly, and fairly.

KEEPING LAW & ORDER WITHOUT CENTRAL POLICE

In a borderless world, crime won't vanish—it will just change shape. Hackers may steal wallets; bots may cheat systems. So instead of one central police, we'll have Security DAOs—community-run justice groups.

If someone is hacked, their case gets reported to a network of DAOs. A jury of global citizens is selected to review the case, using advanced tools that can prove guilt without exposing private details.

Punishments are fair and step-by-step. First, the hacker's wallet can be slowed down. If they continue, their funds can be frozen until a final decision is made. And all cases can be appealed to a Global Arbitration DAO, so justice feels balanced, not biased.

This way, safety still exists—but it comes from community trust, not government fear.

PROTECTING PEOPLE WHO CAN'T ADAPT

Not everyone can live fully digital. Many elders, poor families, or less-educated people may struggle. In a fair decentralized world, they cannot be left behind.

There should be a basic income fund that gives every verified human a small safety cushion. Old people should have easy wallets—big fonts, voice commands, local language, even feature phone support.

Cash should still be accepted in some places, with kiosks to convert it into digital money when needed. And people should be paid to learn step by step, earning small rewards while they finish mini-courses on how to use blockchain safely.

Most importantly, essential services like food, water, medicine, and transport must stay accessible to everyone—even those without digital skills. This ensures freedom doesn't turn into exclusion.

FAIR AND TRANSPARENT GOVERNANCE

Rules should never feel like they're forced. Local issues can be decided quickly by neighborhoods, but bigger changes should need more time and more votes. Rich people shouldn't dominate—systems like quadratic voting give more power to many small voices instead of just a few big ones.

Every new proposal must include a plan for failure: what happens if it goes wrong, who will be protected, and how refunds will be made. That way, trust stays strong.

BUILDING THE RIGHT CULTURE

Technology alone is not enough. People must learn how to live in this system. Schools should teach digital civics—how to verify, how to avoid scams, how to recover when something goes wrong.

Cities should run practice drills—simulating hacks or outages so that people know how to respond calmly. Transparency should be normal: leaders explaining openly when something failed and how it was fixed.

The culture should celebrate truth and fairness more than profit.

THE RESULT

If we design carefully, decentralization will not feel scary. Mistakes will be fixable, justice will be fair, and even the slowest person will not be left behind. The future will be both free and safe—a system without corruption, but full of compassion.

FULL DECENTRALIZATION = (TECHNOLOGY × ADOPTION × AWARENESS) ÷ RESISTANCE

2035: A DAY IN A FULLY DECENTRALIZED WORLD

7:00 AM – Aarav wakes up and checks his Metaverse real estate investments. His smart AI assistant automatically adjusts his crypto portfolio.

10:00 AM – He attends a DAO governance meeting, voting on new policies for his blockchain-powered city.

1:00 PM – He pays for lunch with Bitcoin, using a privacy-focused wallet that government agencies can't track.

3:00 PM – His AI tutor teaches him quantum computing, giving him an NFT-certified skill badge.

6:00 PM – He plays a Play-to-Earn Metaverse game, making ₹50,000 in crypto within a few hours.

10:00 PM – His smart home automatically trades excess solar energy, earning him passive income without lifting a finger.

For Aarav, life is fully automated, borderless, and free from centralized control.

But is this the perfect world?

Or does decentralization bring new challenges that humanity must solve?

THE FINAL QUESTION: IS FULL DECENTRALIZATION POSSIBLE?

YES, IF...

- ❖ Governments embrace blockchain-based governance models.
- ❖ AI & smart contracts become highly secure and error-proof.
- ❖ Financial & legal systems evolve to support decentralized ownership.

NO, IF...

- ❖ Governments fight back with strict regulations and centralization tactics.
- ❖ Cybercrime & hacking make blockchain systems vulnerable.
- ❖ Society resists a world without traditional safety nets.

The truth?

The future isn't fully decentralized or fully centralized.

Instead, the world is moving toward a hybrid system, where decentralization coexists with governance, ensuring both freedom and stability.

The question isn't whether decentralization is possible.

The question is:

Are we ready for it?

******

BEYOND THE HORIZON – YOUR ROLE IN THE DECENTRALIZED REVOLUTION

> *"Blockchain technology isn't just a more efficient way to settle securities. It will fundamentally change market structures, and maybe even the architecture of the Internet itself."*
>
> *– Abigail Johnson, CEO of Fidelity Investments*

The journeys you've taken through this book is not just about technology, money, or digital systems. It's about something far bigger—a shift in the story of humanity itself. For centuries, our world has been organized around centralized powers—kings, empires, banks, governments, and corporations. They held the keys, and the rest of us had to play by their rules.

But history is full of moments when that order was challenged. When printing presses spread ideas beyond the control of monarchs. When electricity and telegraphs connected people across oceans. When the internet opened a new frontier that no single authority could completely control. Each of these shifts redefined what it meant to live, work, and dream.

Now, decentralization is that next great shift.

It is not just about Bitcoin or Ethereum or DAOs. It is about changing the fundamental equation of power. Instead of *few controlling the many*, it is about *many empowering the many*.

Imagine standing at the edge of a vast ocean. Behind you lies the familiar world—banks, governments, traditional jobs, passports, physical borders. Ahead of you lies something unfamiliar, shimmering, and limitless: a decentralized future. It is a horizon where money flows freely without banks, where digital IDs are self-owned, where communities govern themselves without politicians, and where opportunity is no longer tied to where you were born.

This is not a fantasy. It is a direction.

Already, Bitcoin has become a lifeline in countries battling hyperinflation. Already, DAOs are pooling resources from strangers across the globe to build projects bigger than many corporations. Already, young creators in India, Nigeria, and Brazil are earning in crypto, bypassing traditional systems entirely.

We are no longer asking if decentralization will happen.

The only question is:

When—And How Ready We Are When It Arrives.

But here lies the paradox. Freedom always comes with responsibility.

To be your own bank means no middlemen—but also no safety net if you lose your keys. To govern yourself means no rulers—but also no one to blame when decisions fail. To build a decentralized community means no bureaucracy—but also no external force to clean up mistakes.

Are we ready for that responsibility?

History suggests that not everyone will be. Some will cling to centralized systems because they feel safer, even if those systems limit freedom. Others will embrace decentralization, thrive, and become pioneers. The gap between these two groups will shape the next century.

You might wonder—why should I care? Why not just watch from the sidelines and see what happens?

Because revolutions don't wait. The printing press didn't ask permission before changing the world. The internet didn't wait for governments to catch up before transforming business, culture, and communication. Those who embraced the change early became the leaders, innovators, and visionaries remembered in history. Those who resisted often faded into irrelevance.

The decentralized revolution is not just about making money in crypto. It is about reclaiming agency in every aspect of life—how we earn, how we govern, how we express ourselves, and how we connect with others.

If you want financial freedom, creative freedom, or simply the ability to live on your own terms, this revolution concerns you directly.

This book is not meant to simply inform you. It is meant to invite you.

Invite you to learn, to question, to build, to explore. Invite you to stop seeing decentralization as a distant trend and start seeing it as a canvas on which you can paint your own future.

Because here's the truth:

The decentralized world will not be built by governments or corporations. It will be built by ordinary people with extraordinary vision.

People like you.

Close your eyes and imagine the year 2050.

The next generation—your children or grandchildren—ask you about the early days of the crypto and decentralization movement.

What will you tell them?

Will you say, *"I heard about it, but I didn't take it seriously"*?

Or

will you say, *"I was there. I understood it. I became part of it. And I helped shape the world you now live in"*?

History doesn't just happen—it is written by the choices of individuals.

Today, you stand at such a crossroad.

This book began as a journey into ideas—Bitcoin, blockchain, AI, Web3, Metaverse, DeFi. But it ends as something more: a challenge.

Will you adapt—or be left behind?

Will you choose comfort in the old world—or courage in the new?

Will you allow others to decide the terms of your digital freedom,

Or

Will you claim it yourself?

The horizon of decentralization is not miles away. It is right in front of you. The winds of change are already here. The ships are sailing.

The question is simple:

Will you be onboard—or will you remain on the shore?

The revolution is not in 2050.

It is not in some distant future.

It Has Already Begun.

The moment you finish this chapter, the moment you look at your phone, your wallet, your online identity—you are living in the earliest pages of the decentralized era.

And what you choose to do with that awareness will define your story.

Because this revolution doesn't belong to banks, governments, or corporations.

It belongs to you.

******

ABOUT THE AUTHOR

Meet **Subhajit Ghosh**, the author of "*The Crypto Revolution: How Blockchain & Bitcoin Are Changing the World.*"

Subhajit Ghosh is not only a *Crypto Analyst*, but also an Educator, and Thought Leader in the world of digital finance. Holding an MA in Economics and international certifications in Financial Markets (Yale University), FinTech (Wharton, University of Pennsylvania), Blockchain (University at Buffalo, SUNY), and Bitcoin & Cryptocurrency (Princeton University), he combines deep academic knowledge with real-world market experience.

With over *nine years of hands-on expertise* in cryptocurrency trading and blockchain ecosystems, Subhajit has guided investors, entrepreneurs, and enthusiasts through the complexities of this fast-changing digital era.

He is also the author of the popular book ***"The Crypto Investor's Blueprint, The Ultimate Guide to Master the Art of Making Money with Cryptocurrency"*** and the founder of **GrowMoneyInfo.com**, a platform dedicated to financial literacy, blockchain education, and the philosophy of decentralization.

Passionate and visionary, Subhajit believes that *money should empower, not enslave*. Through his writings and teachings, he aims to help people around the world embrace financial independence, unlock the power of blockchain, and prepare for a future where decentralization transforms every part of our lives.

LET'S STAY CONNECTED!

Enjoyed the journey? Continue with my previous book: 📖

"The Crypto Investor's Blueprint, The Ultimate Guide to Master the Art of Making Money with Cryptocurrency"

→ https://tr.ee/twgpZNnGkz

🌐 Explore exclusive content at:

Growmoneyinfo.com

📅 Chat & follow:

Instagram **@su_bha19** | **@Growmoneyinfo**

X/Twitter **@Subhaji43550907**

www.ingramcontent.com/pod-product-compliance
Lightning Source LLC
LaVergne TN
LVHW100255210926
848480LV00003B/928